The Escape Committee

Matthew Button

New Generation **Publishing**

To my parents for their dreams of distant shores
and to our friend Jimmy.

Prologue

Working wipers had seemed important a moment before. One minute I had been fighting valiantly to see through a storm ravaged windscreen, where the glories of the Austrian Alps had been reduced to a blur of earthy greens and brown, the next the fight went out of the steering wheel, the grip left the tyres and without fanfare or warning we were set free of the world of friction and slid sideways towards thousands of vertical feet of nothing.

Time congealed.

There I was clutching the steering wheel of a fifty-year-old car, hunched ready for impact and grimacing the idiot grin of the utterly petrified.

Why had I left the sanctuary of Kufstein that morning?

Why the endearingly old British car?

Why the boot full of Spam, Smash and teabags?

The blame lies in 1967, the Summer of Love, when social barriers were coming down at roughly the same rate that political ones were going up. The Swinging Sixties may have decorated London in its new acrylic technicolours and paisleys, but even this pageantry couldn't shake off the greys and angles hidden beneath, not for two people who had grown up through the Blitz, rationing and conscription. My parents, Pat and Pam, chafed at the confines of post-war London. They daydreamed of the exotic spice laden East with all its charm and mystery.

Throughout my life, stories from their escape had dripped into my soul. On those long boring car journeys or on rainy afternoons of my childhood I heard them over and over again. And now almost fifty years later I'd had the brilliant idea to follow in their footsteps. Sat on the garden steps in the warmth of a Cornish spring, it had all seemed so charming, so exciting and so wonderfully romantic. Swallows flew sorties over my garden and the bantams pottered about the lawn as I decided I would cruise about the highways and byways of a European summer in an old Austin Cambridge just as my parents had done. With one arm hung out of the window, sunglasses in place, I would play with the warm breeze, humming along to their music – Ella Fitzgerald, Dizzy Gillespie, Count Basie and, if it couldn't be avoided, Tom Jones and Cliff Richard. I would be a very cool cat.

Instead everything I possessed had been sodden for weeks. The roads were more like streams. It had rained so often and everything was so damp that I had more chance of growing moss than cultivating a debonair tan.

The root of aquaplaning was buried in my desire for authenticity. I hadn't been content to simply follow their path armed with Mum's dog-eared journals and faded photographs. I had found a 1962 Austin Cambridge, almost identical to the one they had taken, and had escaped from my own mundane life in Cornwall in search of the beauty and adventure of the Sixties.

Yet a month in and I was sliding terrifyingly across the alpine road. If I hit the barrier head on I could look forward to some Austin Cambridge heraldry imprinted on my forehead as it slammed into the steering wheel. If I didn't it was a long fall.

Mum and Dad's adventures had permeated their lives.

And mine, too.

They had struggled through dictatorships and juntas. They had scaled lofty peaks and languished with the lotus-eaters of the deep blue Aegean. There were new friendships, exotic foods and novel experiences, the most extraordinary of which had been the deceased proto-hippy bobbing his less-than-groovy way past their Turkish campsite bound for the Bosphorus and the Med beyond. Not your average scene in Islington. I'd had challenges and incidents aplenty since leaving but where was my exotic adventure? Where were my secret police and camel trains? Where was all the joie de vivre of the Sixties? Where was my dead hippy? Above all, where was my sunshine? Had the EU stripped the world of fun and adventure? Had mass tourism and cheap flights kicked the life out of the continent? Would the EU even be standing as Greeks battled in the streets and the euro teetered dangerously? Could I make it through Syria and into Jordan and succeed where they failed? I had set out to find out for myself and if, by some miracle, the tyres gripped once again, and by the same miracle we didn't hit the barrier and plunge to the valley floor, then maybe I would have my adventure, my exotic intoxication of the East and possibly some answers.

Chapter One – Out of Nowhere

(Charlie Parker)

'D'you think Pat's all right?' asked Ernie as he returned with the round of drinks.

'I'm sure he's fine. Thanks, Ern, mine was the lemonade,' said Pam as another gust shuddered the windows and sent a thick whorl of woodsmoke rolling out of the hearth. It was 1967 and outside the weather was thrashing the Welsh valley, sending the walkers and climbers scuttling for refuge and leaving only the crofters behind in the darkness. She peered through the downpour to see her husband leaping, with less than gazelle-like grace, from island to island across the flooded car park.

'Ernie, shhh! We've moved on from bloody climbing. Now let Pam finishing telling us about her and Pat driving to Africa. Jimmy might go with them,' said Annie. 'How wonderfully romantic, Pam. I'm so very jealous.'

Pat had reached the car and as he busied himself finding the map the pub's bird table, stand and all, pinwheeled through the beer garden. Shoving the map under his arm he attempted to lock the door when a fresh blast tore at the map sending it chasing after the bird table.

Turning back Pam said 'Well, Aqaba in Jordan first,' as she basked in their admiration. Oh, the heady middle-class dream of it all. Pam could leave behind all the friends and colleagues who had surrendered to the imprisonment of motherhood. Nothing could convince her to give up the cars, travel, clothes and climbing that she and Pat had enjoyed since getting married ten years before. She had fitted carpets. They went horse riding in Barnet on the weekends. They were the first in the family to own their own refrigerator, although she played down the fact that they had to share a loo with their neighbours.

'I've wanted to go there since seeing The Snows of Kilimanjaro up at the Odeon. Pat and I are going to quit our jobs and drive east. We're not sure exactly where or how', but she was sure. They had been poring over the AA map for weeks; romance, after all, needs a little planning. 'Pat's been chatting to this Greek lad at the exchange. Can't remember his name, Pat will tell you. Anyway, this lad's been going on about the beautiful beaches and unspoilt Greek country life.'

'You're going where?' Ernie burst out. 'Shit! Isn't there a coop or something in Greece? It was in the papers this morning.'

'Ernie, it's a coup and you don't even know where Greece is.'

'Nor do any of you, Annie,' he retorted.

'No one was questioning your bravery, Ernie, but blimey, what about London?' They all laughed. Jim and Ernie's ice climbing had made respectful ripples

through the climbing fraternity, but on his first trip to London Ernie had wandered the mean streets of Knightsbridge in full mountaineering regalia certain that no thieving southern herbert was going to get the better of a Yorkshireman armed with stout boots, an ice axe and a no-nonsense bobble hat. Here was a man who would dangle from frayed rope halfway up a cliff yet cowered at the horrors of chips and mayonnaise.

Jimmy, however, was keen to get as far away from his engineering apprenticeship as possible and test his mettle in the Alps. His climbing buddy rounded on him incredulously. 'What's wrong with England, Jim? The food is great. No horse meat or snails here, lad.'

'That's France, Ernie, not Greece,' interrupted Pam.

'Who cares? Nought good happens over there, Jim. It's all bombs and foreign buggers cutting off each other's goolies!'

With that the door slammed open and a mud monster stalked menacingly through the crowd and thumped a sodden mass of paper onto the table. 'It's supposed to be bleeding spring! Jimmy are you coming or not?'

'Time you made a cup of tea, son.'

Dad woke me from my daydreams, as he turned off the X-Factor repeat before Mum noticed. The rainy autumn afternoon was dragging on into evening. Soon Mum would pull the curtains across as the last of the day's light gave up.

'It's all right, Pat, I'll make it.' Mum, having finally succumbed to parenthood nearly four decades before, rose. 'Do you want a piece of cake or a biscuit?' I've never been a cake person, not since I have been old enough to make my own dessert related decisions, yet

Mum has remained as single minded as a crack dealer in her offerings of shortbread, fruit slices and carrot cake.

'I'll put the stollen out anyway. Your father will probably eat some.' Pausing at the door she added, 'Pat, did you tell Matthew Jimmy called?' Then she was gone, off to get the cakes of torment.

'You remember Jimmy? James Holmes? Came with us when we took the Cambridge to Turkey?' Not really, I last met him at my brother's christening when I was two. 'She wants you to copy some of those old snaps we took and send him some copies.' It's fair to say that Jimmy couldn't have imagined what a quick phone call to an old friend would set in motion.

I was aware that I had become increasingly tetchy over the previous weeks so, by way of a peace offering, I suggested that Mum dig them out. It was supposed to be a hollow gesture. Dad grabbed his walking sticks and was up out of the chair, calling through to the kitchen, 'Pam! I'll make the tea while you dig out the photos. Have you got your old journals? Matt might like to see them, too.' Turning to me he said over the top of his glasses, 'You never know, you might find in there why you can't sit still for two bloody minutes.'

As the sounds of the British tea ceremony mingled with the extracting of files and boxes from unseen cupboards, I sat in quiet innocence unaware that a touch paper had been lit.

'Here we go,' Mum half placed, half dropped a bursting cardboard box on the coffee table, and with that a landslide of faded transparencies made a bid for freedom. 'We haven't exactly kept them in order,' she said holding one up to the light. A tiny stained-glass image coloured her forehead briefly. 'I think this is Kufstein. What do you think, Pat?'

Returning with the tea Dad put down the tray and had a look. 'Nope, that's near the Scheffau.'

'No. It's definitely Kufstein, don't you remember we stopped to take some photos on the pass?' she said, now armed with her reading glasses.

'Pam, we stopped and Jimmy took photos at every pass. Anyway Kufstein was the campsite we stopped at. Scheffau was near one of the first passes we went through after leaving Germany.' Dad rolled his eyes at me.

'That's right; we were going to do some climbing.'

'No, not in this photo.'

The image went back and forth again. 'Look, the roof rack is fully loaded. We never climbed unless we were camping, so that's why I think it's on the way through Scheffau.'

Nearly five decades had passed, years of children, different homes and holidays were clouding their memories. Only the journals would settle it. As Mum flicked through dog-eared pages I finally had a chance to see the image for myself. Holding it up to the light I could see, captured in faded splendour, two vaguely familiar people, one male and one female, relaxing by a car.

I was dimly aware of having seen it before. Or was I thinking of another trip? There were so many old photos of their adventures in post-war Europe. All my life their stories had drip fed into my soul on long car journeys and rainy afternoons. I remembered the tales of hours of climbing in the clouds, using teabags as currency and of the occasional dead body floating past.

Looking again at the photo framed against the lamp there was something in those faces captured in the muted tones of '60s Kodak glory. On the left, looking cheerful, content and even a little smug, is Mum. She's leaning against Dad affectionately. He's looking pretty smart and dapper. The third member of the group, unseen, is Jimmy. In this image Dad is a man of style and panache, which grates strangely against the Dad I know at home. 'Oh, your dad was always pretty smart and he had such beautiful hair,' said Mum. Was it my fault? Mine and my brothers'? Was there a correlation between the arrival of children and his slow decline into fashion criminality?

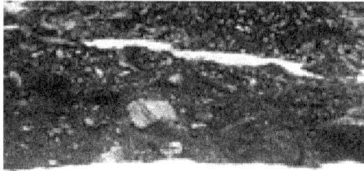

In 1967 as they stood messing about in front of the camera they couldn't have known that their trip would set off a chain reaction that would see them travel as far and wide as they could and eventually passed on to me, along with green eyes and gappy teeth.

I wandered as far as my feet would take me along the Cornish coast and even once I escaped to university I kept gazing at the horizon just as they always had.

Almost immediately upon arriving at uni I began to chafe at the confinement of Stoke's inclement winters and even with all the glories of university life I still couldn't wait to leave. During my final year, as my peers decorated their walls with Ned's Atomic Dustbin posters mine had unconsciously begun to mirror Mum's office walls before they left in 1967. The Wonder Stuff and Dinosaur Jr. were replaced with clippings from Thomas Cook brochures and strip-mined surfing magazines.

At the first opportunity I had left to blood myself in the search for a life less ordinary. I'd had to go to the dusty and unloved corners of the world to get the same sense of excitement and the exotic they'd had on their early trips. I'd ridden through hidden valleys with Kyrgyz nomads, hitchhiked through Iran, and even paddled dugout canoes along the Sepik in Papua New Guinea in search of salt-water crocs; why would I ever think of Europe? I had a slightly jaundiced view of our neighbours. Surely there was no adventure left there? Certainly not on the scale my parents had found in a continent still shrugging off the Second World War. Their Europe had a Germany still divided, an Iron Curtain pulled tight, a malevolent Cold War contrasted against the radiance of the Summer of Love. Today, gilded by Brussels uniformity, it's all mass-tourism and all-inclusives as far as I was concerned.

'Somewhere between Kufstein and Scheffau,' they eventually concluded. But I was still taken with the image. There was a fascinating look of excitement and joie de vie about them. Their calmness and confidence radiates through the way they stand in that snowy mountain car park in July.

'The car was still clean,' he pointed out. 'And so are we. By then we were into the second month of the trip.' They were road fit but not yet road weary. At this point the niggles and annoyances of camping had been sanded away by the joys of movement and freedom.

In the corner you can see their car, a brand new Austin Cambridge A60. It had been the perfect beast of burden, carrying them from the grey streets of Islington to the azures of the Austrian Alps. There was no reason yet to believe it wouldn't carry them all the way to the bleached boulevards of Aqaba in Jordan. Jimmy was adamant that they shouldn't clean it. He wanted it to gather that respectable patina of grime from the open road. It should become a badge of honour and return home caked in experience and the exotic. 'He went mental when I washed it in Thessaloniki,' Dad chuckled.

As I flicked through Mum's half typed, half handwritten notes I began to drift away. Fogged by a mix of envy, excitement and nostalgia the first glimmers of an idea had begun to settle. I had very clear preconceived ideas of travelling in Europe – it was for Interrailers, second-homers or two-week package tour cattle. Then again, I'd had preconceived ideas about many of the places I'd visited and in each case I'd been wrong. Was there any adventure left in Europe? Surely there was nothing left to see or do. Then again…

Maybe I could drive to Aqaba as they had planned. Maybe I could take their journals and photos and retrace their steps. It might tell me a little more about who my parents are and were. Or about me for that matter. Yes, yes now we're thinking. What I needed was a car. Not just any car, but the car. Perhaps if I got hold of an Austin Cambridge from the same period…along with the diaries and photos…then maybe, just maybe, we had the beginnings of a very exciting plan.

Mum was studying me intently. I wasn't sure exactly when they'd stopped talking but now they were looking at me with concerned expressions.

'How much do you think it would cost to buy a car like the one you had?' I asked innocently.

Chapter Two – These Foolish Things
(Billie Holiday)

Pam smiled to herself as she began taking down the glossy photos. On the walls around her desk her daydreams were frozen in images from magazines and brochures. The wall was a tableau of the very best the Greek tourist board had to offer in 1967. With the meticulousness of a lepidopterist each specimen had been pinned to the wall; a montage of heaven as she and Pat saw it. Each was a doorway to a sacred, special, but above all warm, world. Now with exquisite pleasure she pulled out the pin that held the Acropolis captive, looking at the ruin as it lounged high above Athens.

Each icon was bathed in glorious sunshine. Down came the Parthenon, Delphi and the Temple of Apollo. Down came the Evzoni guards, the meze and the dolphins of Knossos.

Pausing, she smiled again, and then threw the lot in the bin.

London, swinging or otherwise, could whistle.

My parents had spent months planning for their lazy sojourn across the continent. They cloistered themselves away in Yorkshire pubs and London bars. Like the escape committees of the prisoner of war camps they worked in secrecy. Easter came and went and the three of them still hunched over maps spread out on tables or living room carpets. They would quit their jobs, take the ferry to Belgium and make their escape. They all agreed that they were going climbing and not, as it would turn out, lounge about in the sun having a whale of a time.

In 2011 things were moving along at a terrifying pace. Having told the world that I was going to take Mum's journals and, as truthfully as possible, follow their journey, I chose to consummate the deal by handing in my notice. With that simple action the reality of it cantered wildly towards me.

Finding an authentic Austin Cambridge for the trip was turning out to be far more difficult than I ever imagined. As I got increasingly desperate Dad had suggested that we start combing vintage car rallies. Each time we pushed through a turnstile and squelched across some boggy field I hoped a few jolly fellows would point me in the right direction. All we had to show for it was a collection of sodden brochures, muddy shoes and rising panic.

'Are you sure it's a good idea?' which was, of course, Dad code for 'I'm sure it's not a good idea.'

As the world staggered into the economic crisis, and Europe, in particular, flailed around on its back like a dying cockroach, it seemed daft beyond words to give up a steady job and head off travelling. After all, like most people I had a mortgage, car and life to worry about.

'I know you weren't happy there, but a job's a job. It's secure work. Not something to be sniffed at in this county.' He handed over his entry fee.

'I sound like your granddad,' he said, a little saddened 'Your mum's dad never really recovered from the Great Depression. It seemed to have affected him worse than the Blitz. He was always asking, "Have you got enough work?" He'd ask us three or four times an hour, just to check. He went mental when we jacked in our jobs. It utterly baffled him. He just couldn't understand it. He thought we were barmy. We always thought he was a daft old sod. After all a few years later it would be very fashionable.'

Mum and Dad had selected an Austin Cambridge A60 Countryman because all three of them, plus their mountains of camping gear, would fit in. For months I had been rummaging through the classic car magazines looking for one. Handing in my notice and buying a ferry ticket before I had a car seemed perverse. The Austin was the most integral part of the journey.

As each month's magazines were thrown in the recycling under the sink, the enormity of the task seemed to grow. What were the chances of finding a classic car not only of the correct age and make, but one that was in good enough condition to carry me thousands of miles across Europe? And one for around £2000?

It seemed an unfeasibly tall order.

Time was ticking away.

I was beginning to lose sleep over it.

There had been a couple of immaculate examples and while they looked flawless in the postage stamp sized photo, they were often double what I could afford. Not to mention that Staffordshire was too far away for a look under the bonnet. I turned to the Internet. Mister eBay and Google hadn't been able to help. When I heard nothing back from the owners' clubs I had even gone as far as pleading on Facebook…but nothing.

Dad and I wandered through the drizzle and endless rows of cars. The grounds had now filled with Pontiacs and Cadillacs, Renaults and Rovers, Morgans, Morrises and Mazdas, MGs galore and Triumphs by the ton but sadly no Austin Cambridge A60s.

To distract himself Dad said, 'I had one of these as soon as I got out of the army,' as he gently touched the wing mirror of an MG. 'A lot changed after I got out.' He had grown up the youngest of eleven kids in a tenement in the grimy Islington. Only nine of the kids survived and when the Second World War had engulfed Europe, Dad and his sister Mary had avoided evacuation by clambering out of a toilet window. They lay low on a bombsite for the day then headed home for tea. He hadn't been so lucky when his conscription papers came through. 'I'd only ever been to Southend,' he said. 'One year you're paddling about in water so dirty you can't see your feet and the next you're in the jungles of Malaya shooting at blokes you can't see.

That certainly opened my eyes. I couldn't have pointed to Singapore on a map. The guy next to me on the ship thought it was somewhere in Norfolk.'

I let Dad have his moment with the MG. 'When the rotten sods let me out they paid me in Scottish pound notes. I couldn't get anyone to take them. Still after that there was to be no more bombsites, no ten kids to a room and certainly no Southend. Thankfully your mum thought the same.'

The MG's owner wobbled our way with a frown and as Dad spied him, he mumbled, 'Christ he'll need a shoehorn to get in this.' We laughed and left to look for the Austins, or at the least something to eat.

'I'll get these,' Dad said, 'you'll be unemployed soon.'

As a local school jazz band cheerfully murdered Charlie Parker's Yardbird Suite I overheard the Jaguar owners discussing last year's jaunt to a rally in the south of France. Next to them the TVR buffs reminisced about an outing to Ipswich.

The tremulous jazz followed us about the grounds. After hours of dead ends and a disappointing roast pork roll, Dad and I gave up. It was at this point, just as the sun threatened to come out, that an immaculate Countryman pulled onto the grass and nearly knocked Dad off his feet.

With a little jig of self-preservation I stepped aside before I pounced on the dapper old driver. I made my introductions and explained my scheme.

He fixed me with an imperious frown and answered pitilessly, 'There are only three working in the country and I have two of them, now if you don't mind I'm off to get a cup of tea,' and with that I was dismissed. I didn't know whether to grab the pompous old shit and shake a civil answer out of him or simply curtsey deferentially. We watched him stride away. I looked at

Dad; he smiled kindly. 'Well, son, that's you fucked. Wanna lift home?'

The big question was whether I should buy a wreck or not. The theory was sound. I would do it up and in the process miraculously transform myself from the mechanical moron the world knew me to be into a maestro who could laugh in the face of all roadside mishaps. Alternatively I could buy one in working order and take my chances.

'Buy a decent one,' said Don without hesitation.

Dad's neighbour, Don Tremayne, was one of those mystical individuals who knew what to do once the oil has been checked and the tyres kicked. He knew about manifolds, sprockets and where to find the engine sump. Don had built and raced cars of every shape and size, but more impressively he had hand built a Jaguar Mark 2. 'A 1960s Austin Cambridge in good enough condition to get you to Turkey but ideally Jordan for about £2000.' He pushed back his cap and frowned. To be honest, if Don had said that it was impossible I would have been back at work on Monday morning on begging knees.

Publicly I had been getting really uptight about not finding a car, but on the inside every day that passed without one gave me a shiver of relief. The reality of the task ahead had begun to sink in. Had I really agreed to take an antique car thousands of miles across Europe bound for the always-frisky Middle East? What the hell was I thinking?

The Six Day War had barred Mum and Dad from entering the Middle East, yet it was the outbreak of peace that looked worryingly like it would scupper my plans. Firstly, Tunisia decided it had endured enough of tyranny and stood up, followed quickly by Egypt. Then from Mauritania to Oman the flames of protest ignited. After Tunisia's victory the Yemenis, Bahrainis and, most troubling for me, the Syrians poured out into the streets calling for peace, freedom and democracy. They weren't to get it. The Guardian was already reporting that Syria's security forces had turned on their own people. Demonstrators fled or were gunned down outside their homes. The route through Damascus and beyond was once again stippled with blood.

The distances, challenge and politics of the journey were too large to comprehend. The newspapers too packed with violence new and old. The TV too chock-a-block with panicked markets as the euro staggered around with each comment from Greece. Maybe Greece would be engulfed in its anti-austerity riots and the journey would falter at the Macedonian border. For my own sanity the trip had to be divided up into small digestible chunks. First, it had to be car, food and tent. Only then could it be recession, global meltdown and war.

Then suddenly a little serendipity graced my world. As my notice ticked away I was decreasingly conscientious and so as I searched about the Internet on my lunch break I found myself at a car site I hadn't visited before. Odd, I thought, but I gamely punched in 'Cornwall' and to my astonishment not one but two Austin Cambridges appeared. But wait, it got better, both were at the same garage, West Country Classics, in Penzance, about an hour's drive away, AND both were £2000. I nearly fell off my stool. Surely there was no room for this kind of providence in the real world?

The following day Don and I drove down to meet the ebullient owner, John. 'That's got to be a good three or four thousand miles right?' I nodded apprehensively as Don tapped something and a small cloud of rust rained down. 'Well, the blue one is most likely to get you there.'

'And back?'

'Maybe?' John laughed.

This was the first time I had actually had a chance to touch and sit in a Cambridge. Now I had a choice of two. I asked John about the history. 'Battista Farina was an Italian car designer. His company built everything from Alfa Romeos and Maseratis to the TGI train. Although I'm not sure if he turned up for work on the days the Austins were made,' he laughed. I had meant its ownership history.

The Austin Motor Company was founded by Herbert Austin at the turn of the century. What had started with experiments in automated sheep shearing quickly evolved into automobiles. The company benefited from both the first and second world wars and fuelled by those government contracts of weapons and vehicles, Austin expanded their A40 Cambridge range. First came the A50, crowing its optional extras of a heater, twin-tone horns and even a passenger's sun visor so the missus wouldn't go blind in the watery English sun. Next came the A55, which offered a two-tone paint job and an additional 4mph when floored. By the time it evolved into the A60 the Cambridge had its characteristic tail fins and chrome side strips and infill, giving it a passing resemblance to a trilby. It may have been able to reach 60mph in under a fortnight and promised a near supersonic 80mph with a strong tail wind but above all it could seat three friendly people in the front and do nearly thirty miles to the gallon. Perfect for a lazy jaunt to the Red Sea.

John's pair didn't look as if they would make it to the pub. The maroon one had been unloved for far too long but the other one, with its white panel stripe cutting through the sky blue Farina design bodywork, I thought was beautiful. A bit of a big nose but handsome all the same. I climbed in and wound down the window manually. 'The four cylinders will still give you a top speed of about 80mph, although I wouldn't advise you experiment much in that area. Unless you like pushing cars, that is.'

It was a whole new world in that front seat. The aroma of antique leather and grease wrapped itself around my heart and soul. It was a perfume that I would never have thought I might like, but suddenly, sitting there looking at the walnut panelling and owlish dials, I fell so utterly in love it astonished me. As I changed through the four gears and flicked through the four switches on the dash I was completely smitten.

I could see myself coasting along the Aegean, sunglasses in place, warm salty air pouring in through the quarter lights while my sun kissed arm daggled, with practiced coolness, over the windowsill. I might even click my fingers along as I manoeuvre smoothly into another sweeping vista down the Hellenic coast. Outside the world would sparkle while inside Nat King Cole would croon '…where one relaxes on the axis of the wheel of life, to get the feel of life…from jazz and cocktails.' Oh yes, I could certainly see myself doing that.

John broke into my reverie. 'This one's from 1962,' he said, tapping the headlights. That was a car of nearly fifty years in age. Even my parents' brand-new one had struggled with the road conditions and the distances. I was looking for an elderly car to do in its retirement what it had struggled to do in its youth.

John went to serve another customer just as Don reappeared from under the chassis. Taking me aside he rattled off a list of ailments that needed to be seen to. The only one that I really understood was that there was some welding, which surely meant it was a deathtrap, didn't it? An hour earlier I would have been faking disappointment but after just ten minutes behind the wheel I would have been crushed beyond words. Don looked me in the eye, placed an oily hand on my shoulder and whispered, 'If you don't buy this car you're an idiot. It's as perfect as you're going to get in this world.'

Chapter Three – To the Ends of the Earth (Nat King Cole)

Excerpt from original diary
Sunday 2nd July 1967. Portland Rise/London
Mum gave us all dinner before we left but it was somewhat marred by Michael and Barbara having a row over dinner. We left home at 10:30 after some sad goodbyes.

'For Heaven's sake, Pam! We know what Arabs do to young boys and women,' wailed Minnie. A neighbour had come back from the Great War and he had plenty of tales. 'What are you thinking?'

Pam's mother, Minnie, could not be convinced or consoled over the news that her daughter, son-in-law, her eldest boy Michael and his wife Barbara were leaving the next morning and consequently the room was more quarrelsome than usual. It had been naïve to think that they would get away without another performance.

'And, Michael, what are you thinking, too! Smuggling money out of the country! I didn't bring you up to be a criminal.'

Michael and Barbara paused in their bickering for him to defend himself. 'Mum, we explained. Harold Wilson says that Pam, Pat and Jim can only take out £100 each. Blame him not me. We'll take out another hundred each then we'll be home next Sunday for Christ sake,' and with that he returned to his squabble with his wife.

All three travellers itched to get away from the table, but Pam itched to escape everything. She needed to flee the brown wallpaper of the Victorian tenement with its ceiling roses and mildew. She needed to escape the tide of Tottenham and Arsenal fans that passed the door every Saturday. But above all she needed to get away from the claustrophobia of her mother.

'Well, I didn't vote for the northerner, Michael! He's given away our empire and jumped into bed with the Germans and French! Bloody Yorkshireman!'

There was a cough. Pat passed Jimmy the boiled potatoes as Minnie at least had the decency to pause in her casual racist tirade, but the rest of the meal would, of course, descend into her all-foreigners-will-put-you-in-a-pot-and-eat-you diatribe and before the Angel Delight arrived there would be the usual threats of suicide as an encore.

Cornwall was a glorious, golden world of impending adventure and frenetic last minute preparations. There were two family bags of carbohydrates, one rice and one pasta. Ten cans of assorted mixed meat products popular in post-war Britain, Spam and corned beef to the connoisseurs of today. Two bags of the culinary delight that went by the generic name Pom to my parents, but today that niche has been filled with Smash. 1967 was not a great period in British cuisine. It was still on a downward trajectory that would finally bottom out with cheese and pineapple hedgehogs. To this vitamin packed diet I had added: one pack of liquorice Catherine wheels, one packet of dates, four boxes of powdered soups, a packet of Garibaldi biscuits and some chocolate mallows. Not exactly Fear and Loathing in Las Vegas I'll grant you, but it was as close to the authentic collection as I could get my hands on in time.

Still there was a needling feeling that something very important was missing. Something very, very important.

So with a boot full of unexciting food, an annotated roadmap and a hastily thrown together collection of imperial tools I dashed round to Mum and Dad's to say my goodbyes. 'Mum, I'm not exactly going to Afghanistan!' I said in face of her tears. 'Yes, but you're not exactly going to Tesco either, son,' countered Dad.

Finally, as I turned the heavy steering wheel, Austin and I pulled out of the village and before us lay an unwritten road, stretching, with luck, all the way to the onion domes of the East.

At last unencumbered by all the minutiae of preparation, I was free to feel the road beneath the Austin's wheels and we rolled contentedly through the dappled Glyn Valley. I turned up Nat King Cole's L-O-V-E and clicked my fingers in time as the excitement threatened to make me burst into song.

Complementing the Sixties food selection was the anthology of music bestowed on me by Mum and Dad.

They had never really crossed over to the Beatles and the Stones. Mum, a fan of Ronnie Scott's, never strayed far from jazz. As a result Austin and I drove through Cornwall joined firstly by Nat King Cole then, later, as the road bore us east, Ella Fitzgerald, Dizzy Gillespie, Billie Holiday, Count Basie and countless others I'd never heard of.

The moment I had sat in the car at the garage, even before money changed hands, the car had become 'Austin'. He was an aristocratic old gent. There was nothing 'cool' about him. If he were alive then he would have worn tweed and perhaps been a retired, but slightly bonkers, schoolmaster. Rather than a kick-ass stereo, GPS and ten-inch rims of modern cars he came with only four gears, no ABS brakes and only a token amount of responsiveness. The only 'primping' that would have been acceptable would probably involve a pipe rack.

His worn leather wrapped you in a wonderful perfume of aged luxury and elegance. Driving Austin was exactly how I imagined retirement to be, but while it may have been like sitting in a drawing room of faded glories, driving Austin had something more in common with travelling by barge. Everything was done slowly. Accelerating away from the lights required patience and if braking was necessary then forward planning was needed, in some cases weeks in advance.

Yet he was a pleasure to travel with and so we had sailed the good ship Austin majestically out in the bright sunshine of a Cornish summer bound for lands unknown and adventures aplenty.

The very short turnaround between finding Austin and leaving had been a whirlwind of paper chasing and mechanical nerves. Dad, fully aware that I was a moron, had done his utmost to decant all his years of car know-how into my simple brain.

31

'Okay, this is the fan belt. You'd best replace this and take a spare.' He made me change all the hoses, plugs and points, all of which seemed pretty simple but then he moved on and failed to take his idiot son with him. 'Matt, listen, this is where the unicorn goes. This is the flange-o-scope. It'll need greasing regularly and make sure you oil its nipples twice a week…'

For my part I avoided going round there as much as possible in the mature belief that if I didn't know how hopelessly ignorant and out of my depth I was, then that would be better for everyone.

What we couldn't do was taken care of by the semi-numinous Tony Perry, an utterly unflappable mechanic who went through the engine making the same assumption my dad had made. 'If you take it slowly, do your checks every day and treat him like the old gentleman he is, he'll take you all way, I'm sure. These old cars are built to last.'

Austin and I made it all the way to Salisbury before I broke him.

Pulling over at a service station I noticed that the speedometer wasn't working. A judicial tapping of the dial didn't have the desired effect, nor did a twiddling of the wires, as suggested by the charming inadequate manual. It was near the end of a very long day, I was already utterly shattered, and so I put the problem aside for the evening. What was needed was a campsite. The original plan would have seen me pulling over somewhere in Southampton. I chose, for no reason other than the proximity to Stonehenge, Salisbury, and began braking early.

It was on that first evening that a few of the realities of driving Austin began to dawn. Firstly, due to his desire not to be rushed, it was only vaguely possible to guess what distances would be achieved in a single day. Once Austin reached about fifty a drum solo of knocks and rattles would rise up from the bodywork. With a pulse to match our acceleration the hidden percussionist beat out a rapturous tempo each time we tried to overtake a dawdling caravan. A rim shot from under the bonnet, a timpani from the rear left wheel arch and deep tom tom throb from the gearbox blossomed with a touch of the accelerator. With the alacrity of Sonny Greer, Austin's mechanics kept time with the road until we returned to the serenity of about fifty.

Another unforeseen problem was Austin's weight. Driving a heavy old vehicle without power steering was gruelling. Whether Austin could continue beyond the six hours was neither here nor there; I couldn't. By the time I found a campsite and pulled myself away from the leather seat I was exhausted and as rigid as a flagpole.

After a single day in Austin I ached and complained like an OAP. As I tried to put up the tent I grumbled about the cost of petrol, the politics of today and the speed everyone drove these days. I began to fear I might spend the evening feeding some pigeons and moaning that no one comes to visit. Instead, when I couldn't get the stove to work I strode stiffly through a housing estate until I came to a supermarket and dined on a very unsatisfying curry.

Once I could no longer face the sallow slop that claimed to be chicken tikka masala I continued my pensioner's existence wandering around a lovely, but seemingly closed, town centre feeling tired, lonely and desperately trying to winkle out that memory that had tormented me all day.

I shuffled through the light rain searching for a little divine intervention at the Cathedral of Saint Mary. It may have opened in 1258 but by the time I arrived, sore and soggy, it had closed for the evening. There was no bolt of celestial lightning from the majestic spire to jog my memory, so I put the misgivings down to fatigue and I ambled stiffly back along the River Avon, beneath a ceiling of dripping willows, until I reached the campsite and I passed out in the tent.

In the morning, as the east began to colour with dawn, I packed up feeling as if I had been beaten up by some angry caravanners. A few dips of the accelerator was all it took for Austin to cough into life and wake the rest of the campsite. Opening the gate, we made ourselves scarce.

A few minutes later I pulled into a lane and with no sign of the sun making an entrance, turned off the engine and with it went Ella Fitzgerald. In view of a silent Stonehenge I opened the boot in search of something to eat that didn't need cooking.

The boot of an Austin Cambridge A60 was a sight to behold. There was enough room to smuggle a handful of druids and a wicker man or two. At that moment it was stuffed to the gunnels with everything anyone could think would be useful for a three-month trip. As I opened it there was a clatter of pots that shattered the morning calm. A couple of indignant pheasants tore away over the hedge before the stillness flowed back in with the mist and I sat in silence, eating muesli before those strangely solemn stones. In twenty-four hours I hoped to be in Belgium. What did I know about the place? Not a lot. Alain, my boss in Tokyo, had been from Brussels. He seemed to me the embodiment of sagacity except for his near-certifiable obsession with the flamboyant rockers Kiss, although I doubted the second one was a national characteristic. His advice had been to try the frites with curry ketchup rather than the traditional mayonnaise. Beyond that I knew very little except from the unconcerned bigotry of the British press reporting 'bonkers Brussels demands…' Apparently, over the years the European

Union, and consequently the Belgians by association, have insisted we Brits straighten our bananas, stop smacking our children and refrain from playing darts. But surely a country that gave us such luminaries as Charlemagne, Magritte, Hergé, and, of course, Jean-Claude Van Damme couldn't be as square as all that? But this time tomorrow I would be, with a little luck, in a better position to say.

'You're going where?' asked the car park guard when I stopped for directions.

On that first morning on the misty flats of Salisbury Plain the novelty of the question hadn't tarnished. I answered proudly, 'Jordan, or as near as I can get.'

The attendants shivered in the cool morning air. They glanced at each other, then down at Austin and back to me. The taller of the two spoke to me as if talking to the hard of thinking. 'You do know how far it is, don't you?' 'About three thousand miles as the crow flies,' I replied. Again, that hesitation, that look. 'But you're not flying, mate. You're going in this,' he thumbed at Austin.

His mate, with the morning paper tucked under his arm, went on, 'You know there's a war in the way?' In my opinion it wasn't quite a war but more a brutal suppression of pro-democracy protests, but would that distinction make any difference to those families who'd recently buried their sons and daughters? The protests in Syria had quickly escalated from civil disobedience to an 'uprising' by March and suddenly the only land route into Jordan had slammed shut. How exactly I planned to get from Turkey to Jordan through one of the most agitated periods of the always-agitated Middle East was a problem I hadn't solved yet. All we could do was travel one mile at a time and see what happened. I put Austin into gear and we pulled cautiously out into the traffic and headed back towards

35

the sea for a long day's meander through a roll call of the English seaside towns. We zigzagged along the British coast behind caravans with their comet tails of frustrated locals and families. The bleached light remained the same, never increasing or decreasing, simply flat and leaden. Brighton, Eastbourne and Bexhill had all slipped by, as time seemed to stand still.

Parking at the seafront in Hastings I got out for ten minutes to stretch my legs. Looking back at Austin, sat there alone, he looked completely at home, as if Hastings had remained in the 1960s just as he had. The town had been the favourite of my nan and as far south as Mum had ever been until she met Dad.

I sat on the railings watching the waves suck on the pebbles like a pensioner struggling with a lozenge. I could see why my young Mum and Dad wanted to escape this. How could the concrete confines of the grey south coast, with its barricades of Georgian tenements, compete with the Elysian sparkle of the Adriatic, the Aegean and the Red Sea? I could understand their hunger to escape the monotone seafronts with their Kiss-me-Quick bonnets, saucy postcards and donkey rides. Golden skinned Europeans sashayed elegantly across bleached sand while the British crunched across pebbles and shale in Sunday bests or cowered from the weather in tearooms with nothing more exotic than a saffron bun. Being young was something relatively new. Package holidays would, realistically, have to wait for another decade. As children of the Swinging Sixties how could they settle for the limited horizons of the south coast? Punch and Judy would be abandoned for the wild exuberance of pulsating Greek Syrtaki dancing. Flat caps, hankies and mouldy tweed would be discarded for the liberty of alluring bikinis, shorts and Coppertone. Who would want to plod along on a threadbare donkey when they could water ski the sizzling day away?

Even on that afternoon in Hastings it was hard not to think that there could be any competition. On the surface little had changed. It was July and no one could be seen even taking that very British delight in our temperamental weather – a bracing walk. My own desire to be away to the warmth and excitement of the continent was so overwhelming I climbed back into Austin, turned the key and headed for Ramsgate and our last night on English soil.

The modern world and the Sixties had already showed themselves to be incompatible in more ways than speed limits and fuel costs. The online ferry booking system simply refused to accept Austin as a choice of vehicle. Twice I had been sent back to the first page to start again. Eventually I tried the old fashioned method and picked up the phone. The nice people at the ferry company confirmed that there were no longer any ferries from Dover to Ostend as there had been in 1967 so instead I had booked myself a place on the Ramsgate–Ostend ship.

Hours later it was a little disconcerting to find myself stood in a rainy English campsite, surrounded on all sides by housing estates, as squadrons of parakeets flew sorties above.

'You are taking him to Jordanië? You are a brave man,' said Frank in that nonchalant Dutch way as the parakeets bickered above. He looked appraisingly at Austin as I fought with my stove. His newly collected 'project' MG lay under a tarpaulin on his trailer and we talked about the months ahead. He would begin his restoration as I headed east. His daughter Marije laughed and rolled her eyes when he admitted he'd had a few other projects that never actually got finished. 'Some of them never even got started,' he chuckled.

With two days' worth of chatter threatening to break through the dams of my English manners Frank should have feared for his ears. The loneliness was an element that I hadn't taken into account. For the majority of my travelling life I had made friends, allies and loose associations as dictated by the route and circumstances. Ask my family and they wouldn't hesitate in answering that I enjoy my own company. I would have completely agreed with them but after two days entombed in Austin I was already starting to get a bit of cabin fever.

I had managed to rein myself in and allow them to go to dinner alone. With the stove showing no signs of relenting, I chose to spend the evening wandering through the soggy delights of Ramsgate.

When the Victorian glories of the cliff top promenade began to wane I found a restaurant with wi-fi and checked on the Greek riots and, in particular, the Arab Spring. While Greece had calmed a little Syria saw a demented escalation. As the death toll rose each day the very seriousness of the journey made the

38

mechanical worries pale. At that moment, sat alone after only a couple of days' travel, the magnitude of present events hit me full in the face. How far would I be willing to go to reach my goal? I'd already sacrificed my job and most of my savings, would I be willing to risk my life, too?

In the end I couldn't face dinner or any more appalling news.

In this low state, that nugget of memory that I had been trying to surface all day suddenly came free with a terrifying crash. Oh no, surely I won't have forgotten that?

I shamelessly dashed back to the campsite in a total panic, the political worries in Greece and Syria momentarily forgotten. In the gloom I tripped over my own guy rope and went sprawling across the wet grass. Jumping up I pulled open Austin's door and snatched up my paperwork file from the glove compartment. No, I won't have been that dim, surely?

The ferry was leaving at 7am the next morning bound for adventures beyond the wind-harassed port, yet I may well not be joining it.

I paled as I double and triple checked my paperwork.

There was no doubt about it, I had left my MOT certificate at home, probably on the scanner. Without it I had no proof that Austin had any degree of road legality. This right to be with me, especially in view of the distances we had to travel, had been a question posed by everyone who saw him. What the hell was I going to do? I was attempting to head to a country known for dotting the i and crossing the t. Surely they would want to see all the paperwork, everything imperiously stamped with official tattoos? It was perhaps the least illustrious start in history.

I sat in Austin, head down, drained, lonely and now marbled in rich Ramsgate mud. It would have been so easy to give up and go home. Yet driving Austin had been an absolute delight. Cruising through the Cornish sunshine it had somehow felt right to be there, on that road, on this trip, in that car. Giving up now felt like a betrayal; a betrayal of my parents' beliefs, my own and, strangely, a betrayal of Austin. As the rain drummed out a lazy bebop on the roof the warm comforting smell of Austin's interior soothed my jangled nerves. It was like a warm, friendly arm around the shoulders and a quiet, confident word in my ear, 'Come on, mate, you can't let the buggers get you down. You can't be beaten by a bit of red tape, surely? Where's all that tenacity you are so proud of, that bloody-mindedness that's got you into so much trouble and fun?'

I was off to find whether EU bureaucracy had suffocated adventure and romance and I had nearly fallen at the first hurdle to paperwork. The irony made me laugh and with it evaporated all the panic, fatigue and fear. Surely that would be part of the fun – how far could I get before I was caught or found out? Like a thief I would sneak silently through the EU without having all my paperwork in order. Okay, not exactly the Scarlet Pimpernel but it turned my mood. Only one thing remained to worry me – two days in and already I'd started talking to the car.

Chapter Four – Travelin' Light
(Billie Holiday)

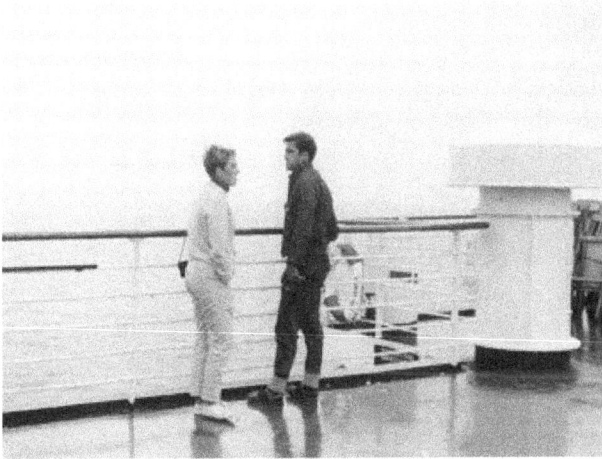

Sunday 2nd July 1967. Portland Rise/London
(After arriving at Ostend)
We took a slow ride down to Dover because the poor car was so overloaded. We eventually arrived at Dover at 12.30pm.
The boat was half empty so we were able to get seats to lay down which enabled us to get a little sleep.

Her husband prowled the deck outside, searching the mist for a first glimpse of Belgium. Michael and Barbara were quiet for a change. Jim napped as Puppet on a String crackled through the PA system.

Her mask of boldness had slipped a bit now that she was no longer defending their decision. There was more out there to worry about than finding a decent hairdresser now. The Third Arab-Israeli War was still all over the morning papers. Who knew if it would flare up again? They were calling it the Six Day War, but no one expected Syria, Jordan and Egypt to take the defeat well.

Who knew if they could enter Yugoslavia? Tito seemed as capricious as he was cruel. Was there anyone left for him to fall out with? The Americans accused him of having Serb and Croat blood on his hands. The borders had only been open since January. How long would they stay open?

What about Greece's new right wing junta? Were they as anglophilic as their predecessors? If not it would be a very short trip. They couldn't go around it to Turkey while the Iron Curtain was drawn so tight. There would be no Slovenia, no souvlakia and no souks. Distractedly she began biting her nails.

She was caught in the limbo between Dover and Ostend and between a crumbling old Britain and the fears of an unknown road ahead. She'd miss Carnaby Street, Mary Quant and her false eyelashes, but not the bombsites and meal times that still cowered beneath the tyranny of a long dead ration book. Safe, dull past or dangerous, exciting future? She looked at Pat leaning on the balustrades watching the sea. He knew which way the wind blew and it wasn't back to the white cliffs.

She'd finish this cigarette and join him outside for some fresh air.

My bravado hadn't lasted. I spent the night in concentrated worry, tormenting myself with obstacles, real and imagined. I fretted about the fidelity of Austin's brakes and his dislike for inclement conditions. Would he turn over after hours on a cold damp ferry? I feared we might need a push just to get into Belgium.

The dull shores of Ramsgate had evaporated into the greyness of the English Channel. We passed a single yacht, a lonesome kittiwake and a trawler with a halo of gulls.

When the mist solidified into the coast of Belgium it was as if we were rising through a dream. My heart began to pound. Europe grew from a thin, notched line until it filled the horizon. This was our cue to leave and the passengers moved to the stairs whilst below the trucks had begun to fill the car bay with a fusillade of noise and fumes.

Frank came over, shook my hand and wished me good luck. He had faith that with a little luck I'd make it all the way and promised to follow my misadventures on the blog. Then that was it. I climbed into Austin and checked the handbrake. It seemed to be holding up. Wincing, I turned the key and Austin burst happily into life. Duke Ellington flooded through the car.

Got so weary of bein' nothin',
Felt so dreary just doin' nothin'
Didn't care ever gettin' nothin', felt so low
Now my eyes on the far horizon can see a glow

Austin, Duke and I idled while the clanks and bangs of boarding and mooring up surrounded us. The car bay door juddered and began to open. And there, in that industrial steel frame, Belgium revealed itself, each trembling inch at a time. I wasn't sure what I was expecting, Belgian Waffle Trees or le Canal de Chocolat perhaps, but what greeted me was, of course, a port that looked a lot like the one I had just left.

The Port of Ostend sat beneath the same ashen skies as Ramsgate as we bounced off the gangplank. A handful of trucks and cars pulled out on an empty quay guarded by a single, neat and not overly officious guard who took a glance at my passport and then waved me on. It was hard to think of the Channel as the world's busiest shipping lane.

And so Austin and I pulled out into the topsy-turvy world of continental Europe. I had to immediately rewire my frazzled brain to drive on the right, read signs in French and/or Dutch and interpret the map in English while sitting on the wrong side of the car.

It didn't exactly start well.

At the very first junction, the first real one of the trip, we set a worrying precedent by turning left instead of right. Our fate was sealed and from that moment on the gods of travel would insist on a sacrificial detour before any destination could be reached.

We were looking for signs to Westend, but Belgium is a dichotomy. The south Wallonia half speak a dialect of French Walloon while the northern Flemish half are influenced by their Dutch neighbours. Of course there had been conflicts between the two groups, particularly when French became the national language after independence from the Netherlands. However, by the 1920s Flemish had become the language of the schools and courts in the northern provinces while Brussels became bilingual, and this mastery of languages is something the Belgians seemed to celebrate in every road sign. Everywhere has multiple names. Brussels (English) was marked as Bruxelles (French), Brussel (Dutch) and Brüssel in German, while Ostend was Ostende in le français, Oostende in Nederlands, and finally Ostende in Deutsch (and these are the easier ones; Liège is Liège, Luik and *Lidje* while Mons is Mons in French but Bergen in Flemish). The signs should have been massive yet what was so wonderfully fascinating about them was not the multilingual bedlam but rather the destinations written on them. If you took the A10 it would escort you first to Bruxelles/Brussel/Brüssel then on to Germany and ever east beyond the old Iron Curtain and Asia beyond. The E17 would bear you north into the snows, saunas and aurora of Scandinavia or, if you preferred the sultriness of the south, then the A18 would draw you languidly towards San Sebastian, Côte d'Azur and the mysteries of North Africa. Where in the UK can you see a road sign that points to another country? Our signs point to the exotic euphoria of Totnes, Scarborough or Bognor Regis. I had never noticed it before but it is something lacking in our character that the signs to the port at Ramsgate didn't say Port of Ramsgate 1 mile, Dunkirk 35 miles, Ostend 69 miles. It is our loss.

It had been the breaking down of these borders, and as a panacea for the rabid nationalism that had set first Europe then the world at each other's throats, that was the spark for a combined Europe. A 'kind of United State of Europe' Churchill had put it almost exactly a year after the end of the collapse of the Axis. By 1958 Belgium, France, Italy, Luxemburg, the Netherlands and West Germany had banded together to form the European Coal and Steel Community (ECSC) and the European Economic Community (EEC). It was to be the seed for a nascent federation of Europe, and eventually the European Union. Still, there was a long way to go. Britain and the rest of Western Europe would have to wait until 1970 to join and even then there was little true unity yet, no true nucleus to this embryonic life form, but at that moment there were only three languages to confuse things; by the time Austin and I drove the wrong way up the coast there would be twenty-four.

While staring up at these beguiling signs we had made a wrong turn somewhere and Austin and I were seemingly half way to Norway by the time a very kind Flemish girl pointed us in the right direction. 'You want Westende? That's south. This is Oostende. You are driving north.' She laughed cheerfully. I swerved nervously across three lanes of traffic and headed back to Ostend's labyrinthine city centre.

It had been a decade since I had visited Europe and I was as pleased as I was overtired. Now heading in roughly the right direction I rejoiced a little. There was such a delight at finding myself in a new country that, had I not been so intent on reading signs and not ploughing into innocent Belgian folk, I would have honked cheerfully all the way back to the city centre. Belgium had seemed superbly new, exciting, even exotic in a wonderfully familiar way. I knew a little more about Belgium thanks to my damp evening in Ramsgate. I remember Mum saying that I had been born in the hospital in St Asaph in which Henry Morgan Stanley was born. John Rowlands grew from a pauper to one of the most famous individuals; marching through the jungles of East Africa he found both the source of the Nile and Doctor Livingstone. That was the lighter side of his history; he had also gifted Leopold II the entire Congo and kick started the ruthless scrabble for Africa. The tiny country of Belgium, barely larger than Wales, has gifted the world not just waffles, chocolate, 'French' fries, Rene Magritte and Audrey Hepburn, but also Tin Tin, the Smurfs and apparently Brussels sprouts. It was the Belgian musical inventor Adolphe Sax who, in a haze of artistic fireworks, fashioned the saxophone and without whom Charlie Parker, John Coltrane or Sonny Rollins might have remained little more than gifted whistlers. Thirty minutes into the journey and I could feel my horizons broadening.

The streets were neat and tree lined, but not overly fussy or rigid, straight but with a hint of medieval chaos that separates Europe from the rest of the modern western world. Everyone drove civilly, and much later, if I made it to the fetid bedlam of an Istanbul rush hour, I would undoubtedly thank the gentle Belgians for this introduction to the right hand driving world, but in the meantime I had other problems. When Mum and Dad had rolled off the ferry driving and navigation were divided five ways. Alone I searched for signs to Westende whilst trying not to cause an accident. As I bravely headed into an underpass I could only recognise Bruges and Brussels on the signs. It was then that I realised an almighty flaw in my planning – the middle detail.

Before departure Dad diligently annotated the pages of the map with a highlighter pen; yellow for the route down and pink for the return. The main roads were clear, as was the street detail around the campsite, but the gap between these two scales, one that is easily bridged by modern sat-navs, was completely missing. I had nothing to guide me from the ferry port onwards through the city and eventually to the campsite. It wasn't until I asked a young man with a face like one of Belgium's most wanted that I had any idea I should have been searching for the signs to Middelkerke first.

That lack of foresight did, however, allow me a slow, if mildly traumatic, tour of Ostend's civic splendours. I peeked at the marina with the beautiful *barquentine* Mercator moored in its littered waters. I later learned that the fifteen magnificent sails drew the sleek steel vessel all the way to the Easter Islands, Iceland and even the North Pole. Such respectable feats of navigation stood in stark contrast to my own as Austin and I continued our haphazard detour and passed beneath the glare of Sint-Petrus-en-Pauluskerk's

47

neo-gothic gargoyles. We had a moment to admire the road works outside the Casino Kursaal Oostende. Changing through the gears in time with the traffic lights we had a glimpse of Royal Esplanade, with its inflatable animals, beach paraphernalia and tourist tat, the only signs of summer beneath the heavy skies. Somehow the Mercator went by again, and then the train station and the British styled Leopold's Park with its bronze statue of Dikke Mathile ('fat Matilda') and floral clock. We glimpsed the sea beyond the flanks of Leopold II, riding majestically towards the beach in full military regalia perhaps just having anointed Herbert Austin, later to become 1st Baron Austin, the founder of the Austin Motor Company, the Order of the Crown for employing Belgian refugees during the Second World War. We had a brief moment to wonder whether those Belgians had been crafting aircraft parts in one of Austin's wartime Shadow Factories before we panicked and turned off Konning Astridlaad. The Mercator went by a third time as we pinballed though the sites and roadworks. Then, just as I began to fear we might have to camp in the park, we found ourselves miraculously on a road to Middelkerke.

As Ostend thinned into Middelkerke the number of tourists in town began to concern me. When my parents came this way they had no problems getting themselves accommodation. In the spirit of their adventure and, because of Austin's desire not to be rushed, I hadn't booked any campsites in advance. Naively I had assumed that everyone would happily throw open their doors to my charming and romantic adventure, and that all I needed to do was present myself at their reception at a time convenient for both parties and bingo! I'd be cheerfully hammering in pegs before ambling off to the patisserie for a light lunch.

It was the beginning of the peak season and the volume of families swarming through Ostend had added to my anxiety. I was less than confident of finding the specific campsite and as I stopped at some lights in Middelkerke and forty people and prams crossed I began to believe that I had made a serious error being so cavalier.

In this state of agitation I pushed on south braving the roundabouts and junctions of Flanders without a clue about Belgium's highway code. I was gloriously driving into a world that I was utterly ignorant about and it felt terrifying and delightful all at once. But it was hard to find any superlatives for the miles and miles of flat wetlands of West-Vlaanderen. I had never seen anywhere so flush. The world was skimmed flat as far as the horizon.

I was aware that the North Sea was out there to my right but as we travelled through the polder wetlands I wondered whether we were traveling below sea level. If I had been on the Zeedijk (N34) road, which shadowed the North Sea, I might have been able to say, but instead Austin and I rattled along the far less pronounceable Nieuwpoortsesteenweg (N318) with its intermittent casinos.

As we pressed on, the journey seemed to be taking forever. The Flanders coast, which reaches from Knokke-Heist on the Dutch border to De Panne on the French, is only 42 miles long, yet Austin and I had been driving for nearly three hours. Eventually half an hour later Austin and I pulled beneath the whitewashed archway of the campsite Westende with my nerves a little tattered.

I had wondered whether any of the original places were left. How many of the 1960s campsites or cafés had survived the rise of a single Europe? How many remained small and charming? Or had they been forced to expand or go under in a new world of dictated uniformity? One at least had survived, the Camping Westende. Tired but a little pleased with ourselves we made our way to the reception just as the crew had done in 1967.

I pulled up outside the shower block. The site was utterly rammed. After the emptiness of the wetlands it was jarring. Every inch of pitch was covered in a refugee mosaic of tarpaulin and lightweight fibreglass. Children on every form of bike, roller skate and skateboard careered about like a pissed off wasp's nest. Their parents were crammed between competing barbeques as tournaments played out in the boules park. Great clouds of meaty smoke bellowed over the privet hedge and followed me into the reception.

Behind the orderly counter sat a grey haired man talking hurriedly on the phone. He made no effort to make eye contact as I stood nervously waiting. A certain degree of flexibility was imposed by Austin's many charming eccentricities but as I stood there being ignored I realised that this was where my plans buckled. I had spent three hours driving past countless inviting campsites, just to pitch my tent on the very spot they had in 1967.

I willed him to finish his call while I tried not to think about the consequences of having to turn around. Surely they could fit me in. Handing over one of my prepared postcards I would explain as best as I could that my Mum and Dad, the couple on the postcard, had driven here to this very campsite in 1967 and that I was following their journey in my own Austin Cambridge. He would in turn swoon at the romance at the whole affair and let me stay, probably offering me some free beer, some waffles and complimentary chocolates.

Pausing in his conversation he looked up.

A friend had warned me that speaking French in a Flemish region might result in a punch in the face so I smiled my brightest smile and declared confidently 'Ik rijd deze oude auto naar het Midden-Oosten zoals mijn ouders deden in 1967.'

He looked at me in utter bafflement.

I panicked and tried French 'Avez-vous l'espace d'une tente?' He looked at me with a worrying degree of suspicion. 'Non, nous sommes pleinement' and returned to his call.

They were fully booked.

Merde!

Chapter Five – Things Ain't What They Used to Be (Duke Ellington)

Sunday 2nd July 1967. Portland Rise/London
(After arriving at Westende)
The afternoon was beautiful (90 in the shade) but the heat didn't agree with Michael and Barbara, in fact they said they wanted to leave on Wednesday. Jim, Pat and I went down to the beach and had a dip in the sea. It was wonderfully warm. We then lay in the sun.
Mileage for the day 252   Acc. Mileage 365

Pam put her finger in the page and closed Mountains and a Shore by Michael Pereira and watched her younger brother stalk across the campsite, toilet roll under arm.

'No luck, Mickey?' she asked knowing the answer.

'She's still there! I can't go while she's there. I'm sure she's watching. We have our own loo roll why do we need to pay?' The old lady who guarded the toilet block demanded one franc for toilet paper, but campers

weren't allowed in without purchase. Everyone had been a little indignant but Michael couldn't let it go.

Pam sighed as he threw himself into the shade. He moaned about the heat and the sun. 'That's why we came here,' Pam had said as she patted her shorts, pleased that her Capri pants were finally packed away. He was convinced it was all a device to upset, sunburn and starve him. The metal pipe sticking out of the wall that was the shower didn't have a rose to spray the water. That had distressed him nearly as much as the toilets. Then he ripped off his toenail at the beach playing football and moaned not about the blood or pain but rather about the two francs donation he left at the first aid hut.

Pam wasn't sure it had been a good idea to bring them after all. But they needed the money. Jimmy had his £100, she had hers and Pat had his plus a bit more smuggled in his shoe. She still wasn't sure why Her Majesty's Customs and Excise refused to allow them to take it out of the country; something to do with war debt. The only way to circumvent the problem had been to bring along her brother and his (soon to be ex) wife for a 'free' holiday. Such mercenary activities had come at a surprising price and everyone was beginning to regret it, but the pair would be going home tomorrow, thankfully.

The sun warmed her legs and, smiling, she returned to her book.

This was only the first day and I had failed already. Where was I going to stay? What would be the point of staying somewhere else? I was utterly crestfallen.

So overwhelmed by this I almost missed the young man who stepped into the reception. 'Papa, regardez ça.

C'est magnifique!' and pointed to Austin hidden by a small crowd of admirers.

Glaring at Austin and then back at me he said in English, 'This is you?' With the alacrity of a drowning man I explained the 'Escape Committee'. As the original mission had been planned with the single-mindedness of a wartime escape party it seemed a perfect title for my shining adventure. The family looked over Austin incredulously and asked, 'Vous allez où?'

'Le Moyen-Orient.' This was greeted with the usual looks of incredulity.

'Le Moyen-Orient?'

'Oui, La Jordanie.'

He looked at his son. Both seemed harassed by the peak season and I couldn't tell if it was admiration or a fear that my stupidity was contagious. Fate held her breath, but each appraising thumbs-up from the campers tilted things in my favour. A broad smile broke out on his face and with a 'Oui! Let's find you somewhere small.'

I was tucked in behind a gaggle of Walloon Hell's Angels. The manager made a hand sign that might have meant that they were deaf or alternatively they'd make me deaf, either way I was just glad to be shown my pitch. With a view of an ivy shrouded factory wall, the ball court and the arse end of a row of static caravans it wasn't the dreamy spot I had imagined when reading Mum's diaries but I was so thoroughly and genuinely grateful to be in that I'd have happily camped in a cess pool.

In the twilight I opened Austin's boot to a chaos of repair kits, tool kits, spares, monster bags of pasta and rice and a small library of books. From the safe distance of home I believed that each evening, after a stately day's drive, I would conclude my camp gastronomy and retire with a good book. I had Patrick Leigh Fermor for Germany and Austria; Rebecca Black would look after the Balkans, and Lawrence Durrell, Ryszard Kapuscinski, and some Philip Marsden would take me through Greece and the East.

As a plan it had many merits if utterly lacking in the realities of life on the road with Austin. As panic evaporated fatigue moved in. I dragged myself through the tent assembly. The stove remained adamant that it would not be an active member of the crew and so I rifled unenthusiastically through my vintage larder and selected a tin that didn't need heating and, a little sullenly, crawled into my tent muttering a chain of expletives. I noted in my journal –'The Hell's Angels next door are having a BBQ and Jack Daniels on the rocks. I have corned beef.'

With surprising decorum the Walloons quietly drank their way into the small hours. However, the holidaying kids kept up a barrage of screams and booms as various balls reverberated off the old factory wall in the ballpark. The darling little shits squeezed every ounce of daylight out of the long silver dusk and just before murder was done the last of them drifted away home.

My parents had headed straight for Lombardsijde-Strand and the beach armed with only their towels, cossies and sun cream. I didn't fancy hypothermia so the next morning I gave Austin the day off and decided to have a look at the delights of nearby Bruges.

Pulling on my jacket I let the wind push and shove me along Duinenlaan until I reached the tram-halte and took the clean and modern tram back into Ostend for the day. For the guidebook I learned that the Flanders De Kusttram tramline is the world's longest, stretching almost from the Netherlands to France. Even I couldn't get lost on it and I was content to let someone else drive for the day. The Belgian royals had shone their beneficence on the area and it had quickly developed into a seaside resort for the discerning king and commoner alike. Sadly today the coast between Westende and Ostend is hidden behind a nearly continuous fortification of seafront flats, punctuated in places with an open-air theatre or square.

Exiting the tram I took a moment to get my bearings. To reach Bruges I would have to switch to the train and, fully aware of my language skills, nervously entered the imposing bluestone and granite edifice that is the Oostende railway station and joined the back of the queue.

Any gift for languages I might have had beached itself in the first year at secondary school. A visit to Austria meant I could count to ten in German so I felt this qualified me for Herr Batty's Deutsche klasse. Instead I was put into Mademoiselle Hollow's classe française. This was no loss as she'd had the attention of every boy in her class, but perhaps not in the way she and the Local Education Authority would have hoped for. Within minutes she became adamant that my linguistic abilities best suited the pursuit of German, while Herr Batty was equally vehement that my talents lay in the Francophile world. Eventually everyone agreed I should avoid languages and do three sciences.

In view of my linguistic magnificence I resigned myself to the ritual humiliation of Englishmen attempting le française. I mumbled 'Un billet à Bruges, s'il vous plait' as I watched the gamine young lady behind the counter. She cheerfully dealt with each of the six sodden customers ahead of me, effortlessly switching between French and Flemish, then German and Italian before addressing me in perfect English. To a man who once gave his age in Japanese as 'strawberry-years-old' this bordered on the supernatural.

Everything was utterly amazing and wonderfully European. The languages were so beguilingly close yet amazingly mysterious; was a Waterzooi something you put ketchup on or found in an aquarium? It would all be brilliant I was sure. People sat around in cafés smoking and drinking coffee strong enough to remove tooth enamel. Bruges has been on my doorstep all my life. At any moment it could have been a mini-break. It had been good enough for both the first and last Yorkish Kings of England and for Charles II on the run from Cromwell's Roundheads, but until I left the train station you couldn't have persuaded me to visit even if Angelina Jolie was up for a dirty weekend. Yet I spent a wonderful morning dodging rain showers, conga lines of tourists and horse drawn carriages as I ambled through the medieval lanes and peaceful parks. The weeks of brain boiling preparation and the stress of the first days evaporated as I pretended to be looking for a new stove but instead found myself lost in the beauty of the Saint-Salvator Cathedral or the whitewashed alms houses, or some other charming diversion. I was as easily distracted as a kitten in a wool shop.

As I wandered aimlessly my feet migrated leisurely towards the Markt. On that second day even the tourist tat cheered me up. My partner Nicole had just scored a new job but felt it would be a little tactless to immediately ask for three months off to drive across Europe and Turkey so had remained at home. To compensate and bring her a little esprit du voyage she very nearly found herself the recipient of a Manneken Pis bottle opener. Although in the end I waivered and decided a pissing infant and alcohol sent out the wrong message and went for the safer option of Belgium chocolate.

When I began to get a little overawed by the neo-gothic glories, I settled into a café in the shadow of the

Belfry and wrote my blog and spilled coffee in my lap whilst doing my best to pass as a literary ponce.

Framed between the grey heavens, gargoyles and flèches of the Markt flew the golden halo of the EU flag. After a lot of bickering, and Europeans can certainly bicker, about the design and the number of stars Belgian Paul Lévy and Frenchman Arsène Heitzhad fixed a constellation of twelve stars against an azure sky. It was at the port and next to every Belgium flag I had seen during my zigzagging through Ostend. The Belgians seemed as proud of the EU flag as of their own flag, yet the only place I recall seeing it regularly in Cornwall was on notice boards next to the word 'funding'. In daily life the only other reference to the EU would be the xenophobic rubbish that periodically turns up in the British press. Daily Mail, that bastion of scaremongering, had listed the EU as one of the causes of cancer, along with immigrants, Prince Philip (although that I would believe) and fizzy pop. The 'Bonkers Brussels Bureaucrats' are even blamed for the standardisation of apples, cucumbers and condom lengths. They have been falsely accused of wishing to outlaw smacking, A-levels, Cheddar cheese and bath time ducks.

It is impossible for someone my age to remember a time before the EU, but in 1967, just two months before Mum and Dad departed, Harold Wilson put in a second application to join. The first had been turned down in 1952 when the French and Germans, fearing that the British weren't taking it seriously enough and that they were too closely allied to the Americans, vetoed their submission. It would take a few more years but by the time the paperwork had been done De Gaulle, the most vocal of member of the opposition, was out of power and the Pompidou government invited the British,

Austrians, Danes, Norwegians, Portuguese, Swedes and the Swiss to join them in Brussels.

Since then the EU has blossomed, or distended, depending on your view, to twenty-seven member states with twenty-three official languages and a permanent representative at the UN. Since 1995 it's had its own currency, the euro, which is second only to the mighty US greenback in reserves and circulation. Although depending on the outcome of crisis talks, Greece might then have brought it all crumbling down again in a single riotous summer.

But Greece and its tribulations seemed a long way from the civilised and soporific air of Bruges' Markt. I could have stayed there all summer switching from coffee to one of the 350 varieties of beer available in Belgium, but after making a promise to bring Nicole here sometime in the winter (I couldn't think of anything more romantic than walking across these cobbles under a brittle winter sky) I decided to make my way back.

With thoughts of home my mood deteriorated as I watched the North Sea through the gaps in the seafront palisade. When I got off at my stop the coast was still veiled in thick bitter mist. It felt as if autumn was making a grab for July before summer had even squared its shoulders. In no hurry to return to the loneliness of the blue grey world of the tent I walked along the Koning Ridderdijk promenade searching for some fresh fruit to supplement my 1960s diet and stave off scurvy.

Leaning on the ballistae looking out along the elegiac coast it seemed neatly divided up into equal sub-beaches, each retained within a stone groyne. The info booklet in my pocket briefed me on where I could walk my dog, swim, surf, windsurf and ride a horse. Each beachlet had a sign informing what I may and may not do, even what to do if I wanted to fish from a horse. Having grown up in Cornwall where the sea does whatever it wants and so do the locals, it all seemed, if not futile, then over officious. Maybe here on this small scale, as the gales sandpapered my cheeks, was an example of Belgium with all its straight lines and rules that I could understand.

It brought me back to the problem of the missing paperwork, official dockets and the rising list of mechanical faults. Maybe it was simply my spirits but the comprehension of the task at hand and distances ahead seemed unimaginably far and the end goal beyond reach.

Leaning against the wind I glanced between gusts up and down the seashore. Mum and Dad's time at Ostend had been a sun filled Elysian daydream, a chance to relax and revel in their decision. Dad had reminisced about 'gingerbread houses' lining the coast and golden beaches empty except for a few families. 'Southend was like playing in icy stale gravy, but

Belgium was bliss,' Mum had said. Today the campsite is encircled by development but the barricade of beach flats thankfully peter out at Westende leaving the last dunes to curve away south towards Dunkirk and France.

The softness of the muted sky contrasted against the harshness of the sea. The view was so utterly unrewarding that I decided to join the cheerfully brave patrons of one of the cafés. Coffee wouldn't be breaking the Sixties tinned meat diet and so I pushed through the door and took the last table sheltered behind the plastic fortification amongst storm refugees. My French drew a pained wince from the waiter. He turned and disappeared back into a warm world of hidden kitchens and people without coats on. Each time the door opened the clatter of plates and pans escaped along with the hiss of espresso machines.

A tall man with a neat goatee indicated he would like the spare seat at my table. He laughed and replied in English, 'Your French is horrible, so you must be English.' It seemed a fair enough comment. Jan joined me as I warmed my hands on my coffee. 'I think your schools teach you like this just to upset the French nation.' Jan was combining a little business and pleasure. A geomorphologist by profession he was surveying the coast. He talked of sand nourishment schemes, granulometric analysis and tidal oscillation, all of which translated to the fact that the Flemish coast was eroding at a distressing pace and with only forty-two miles left the government was keen to keep as much as it could. The seafront, exposed to the aggressions of the Channel, moves Flemish sands a tiny distance into France each year. I thought that surely meant Belgium would gain a little from the Netherlands, and the Netherlands from Denmark. While he talked about the staggering €300m ('Or maybe drachma if the Greeks keep going') project to prevent the damage, I smiled, liking the idea that the geography, as well as people, of the EU moves about freely. Ostend was, a few grains of sand at a time, migrating south. I told him this and for an instant I thought he might be offended by my flippancy, yet he laughed and ordered a cappuccino and asked why I was here.

His father too had come here after his final tour of the Belgian Congo. Both our fathers returned to Europe from corroding empires. The Belgian colonial empire collapsed with the independence of the Congo while the British Empire crumbled, nations flaking off with each passing year. 1967 saw the departure of tiny Anguilla, but the year before had seen the loss of Barbados, Lesotho and Botswana.

'My father used to come here with my mother when there was nothing here,' he said. 'He always talks of those times, of the deserted beaches and simpleness but now he owns one of these ugly maison de vacances,' and he nodded upwards. Above, the flats were stacked high into the milky skies like a giant's bookcase. On warmer days their balconies would be hung with the heraldry of beach holidays, the flags of beach towels and pennants of bikinis and shorts, but today only gulls hung in the breeze. Sheltered from the wind the bouquet of dinners blended with the cigarette fumes and my stomach rumbled. If I gave in to temptation and abandoned this ridiculous diet of Sixties tinned and powdered crap, with just a pathetic placing of a finger on the menu I could be up to my snout in Moules et frites, *To*mate-crevette or Gegratineerd witloof smothered in béchamel sauce crowned with cheese. This thought didn't lighten my mood.

While we waited for his food to arrive Jan attempted to unravel the riddle of Brussels for me. Like most

British I believed the city to be the capital of the EU, but apparently it is only just the de facto capital. The EU doesn't plan to have a centralised capital. Initially Belgium scored a home goal after backing Leige rather than Brussels, then there was a bid for dominance by Strasbourg, Luxemburg and partially Edinburgh. Eventually the Belgians got behind Brussels. There was a nasty incident involving 'abstinence' (I think Jan meant asbestos), Leige seems to have been sent off, which paved the way for a strong Brussels push, there were allegations of unsportsmanlike behaviour (from the Scots?), massive government investments and when the final whistle went Brussels came out on top holding the majority of the European institutions, including the European Commission and NATO. Luxemburg got to keep all the dull things like the European Court of Justice and the European Court of Auditors, Strasbourg got to keep the European Parliament and the Council of Europe while Edinburgh, I think, got to keep the dog and the rubbish CDs. Just as I was beginning to think it would take me the entire trip to understand it all Jan's dinner arrived and I was faced with the duel challenges of unravelling the Gordian knot of the EU and the aroma of a fresh cooked meal of Vlaamse stoofkarbonaden, Flemish beef stew.

It was all too much so I made my excuses and left before I attempted to assail Jan with his own spoon and flee with his mayonnaise shrimps. Almost immediately I regretted leaving the warm companionable atmosphere of the restaurant and as the sand peppered my skin the smells of the meal tormented me. I ambled disheartened back to the campsite, *pâtisseries* taunting me all the way, for another night of Sixties culinary enchantment.

Turning the corner at the toilet block I found, parked behind Austin, a Rover 220 Diesel painted in matt red oxide paint with blackboard paint on the doors and bonnet. Down the side was daubed a very emaciated hamster and the legend 'The Brassic Sparks'.

'It's supposed to be a dinosaur,' laughed the young English driver.

'Those guys,' he said thumbing at the Ford Escort in front 'are the Persistent Planks. That's Joe and Harry. I'm Kieran.' We looked at the Escort. 'They painted it orange to look like a tiger.' We looked at it again.

'But it's yellow,' I said.

'Well…they've been telling everyone that it's a yellow taxi, but we all know it was supposed to be orange.'

Squeezed around the back of the static caravans my new neighbours were merrily bickering and putting up their tents with the polished air of people who knew what they were doing. 'We've been together three weeks now,' Kieran explained 'and we're all a bit fed up with each other.' It didn't look like it to me. 'That's not true,' corrected Angela, 'we're all a bit fed up with Harry.' They all laughed and I envied their company, camaraderie but particularly their working stove.

The four had been having a blast over the last few weeks of mischief and misadventure. In Spittal, Austria another team had put a frog in Joe's bed 'It was a toad!' the others chorused.

'Yeah, but I got revenge on them,' Harry went on. 'I smeared hotdogs all over their windscreen, up the exhaust and in the engine.'

He beamed with pride and solidarity.

'Shame it was the wrong car,' said Kieran.

They had blagged their way into the Milan Stadium for free, sneaked into the Red Bull racetrack in Spielberg and made Harry swim in Lake Zurich in just a mankini. 'You should have seen his face when he

tried to get out and found a small audience waiting.'
They roared with laughter.

As the evening darkened my spirits lifted.
Obviously I was going to have low days. The distance
from my family and Nic, the monotony and cabin fever
of long drives and the pressure of doing everything
alone was obviously going to get me down periodically,
but as I sat with the Brassic Sparks and Persistent
Planks, drinking tea and listening to their adventures,
the ghosts of my parents' trip could be seen and heard
on the edge of their tales. It was a wonderful wake up
call and exactly what I needed.

Later, as I lay in the darkness of my tent half
listening to the lullaby of Walloon bikers singing and
the good-natured squabbling of Kieran, Angela, Joe and
Harry, my heart lightened and the excitement began to
blaze again.

Chapter Six – Ghost of Yesterday (Billie Holiday)

> Friday 7th July 1967. Rottbizte/Germany
> We went back to the tents, changed and had dinner, which consisted of tinned stewed steak, French beans, mashed and sauté potatoes, followed by sago and jam. Quite a meal – all tinned, dried or dehydrated!!!
> Mileage for the day – 218   Acc. Mileage 583

Pam floated, a lone bather crucified against a silver arch of fresh water. From above, the singular glare of the Teutonic sun warmed her skin, while beneath the surface only the distant rumble of a boat reached her ears.

It had been a blistering day. Barbara and Michael had been waved off back to their tedious jobs, Arsenal and spiralling towards divorce. There had been no sign of them on the deck as the ferry pulled away. Why they wanted to go home with its grey skies and rain was beyond her. Maybe it was simply the promise of colour television, but did he really think he could afford one?

The world here and now was more vivid, wild and new and exciting than the BBC surely? But Michael's departure had sparked a metamorphosis and the journey began again with new colours, freedom and life.

Piling their kit onto the roof rack, the trio set out for Germany so excitedly that had it not been for the warning hoots of Belgian Renaults and Citroens then the luggage would have been ripped violently from the roof by the first of many underpasses that bored through Brussels. That had been a narrow escape and now seemed funny, even if it had nearly been a very expensive cock-up. With their confidence checked a little they had progressed through the oppressive heat, the sun gluing them to the leather seats, staring at signs for cities they had only ever heard of in bombing campaigns and Cold War tragedies. Signs pointed them to Aachen, Dresden, Frankfurt, Munich and poor, isolated Berlin trapped behind the Iron Curtain in Trabant-choked East Germany. But like Pat said the Autobahn was perfect, you would never have known there had been a war.

It had been a fun, carefree day full of promise and anticipation. By the time Jim tried to buy some food in the butcher's they were all a little giddy. Controlling a fit of giggles, he had approached the Metzger and with a straight face ordered 'Dry. Worst. Bitter' and to their amazement and amusement they now had sausages for breakfast. It was twice as funny as Pat had lost his temper with a local who attempted to jump the queue, although it would be a while before he found it funny, then again he had done most of the driving while Pam and Jim just watched a verdant Deutschland float by.

Germany would only be a short stop, a passage through to the Alps. There were still no reports on Yugoslavia, only gossip. They guessed that the 'Six Day War' had been only six days after all as there was nothing on the World Service. There were only bulletins on revolts in the Belgian Congo, the Nigerian invasion of Biafra and the formation of the European Communities.

A series of concussions boomed beneath the surface and Pam lifted her head as a swan lifted itself into the now hazy sky. Pat and Jim were at the tent. Pat was bent over the stove as usual. Jim trying to help, as usual. Both laughing at something. She rolled into the cool stillness.

Perhaps no news was good news she thought and, as she chuckled to herself, thought, at least Jim speaks German now.

The susurrations of sleeping campers were the only challenge to the hiss of the drizzle as I packed. I had awoken sore and cold and, although the first suspicions about my tent's integrity were beginning to metastasise, my mood had improved greatly even if the weather hadn't. The damp had seeped into my chest and stifling a cough I wished the sleeping Bratislava crew all a quiet au revoir and set out for Germany.

Austin and I passed out of Dutch dominated Flanders into the Catholic Walloon south, passing Leige/Liuk, the birthplace of Charlemagne, and setting our sights as firmly as possible through the rainy windscreen on Aachen and Cologne/Koln beyond. As Belgium's wooded Hesbaye region receded into the world behind I rummaged around in the glove compartment and pulled out my passport and files. Thanks to the Brassic Sparks I had been reminded of the Europeans' love of tollbooths. Most sensible people prefer to travel with a beloved co-pilot, whether a spouse, wingman (or wingwoman) or homicidal hitchhiker collected from the hard shoulder in a fit of misguided benevolence. The Euro Crisis and the escalation in Syria was so huge as to be almost intangible, but tackling toll booths, alone and in a right-hand drive car, was a problem I could really fret about. At each toll or border I would have to throw off the seat belt, scoot across the seat bench, manually wind down the window, and squirm out simply to proffer my euros and/or my papers. Then, with the speed of a greasy whippet I had to do it all in reverse, pop Austin back into gear and make my getaway. The probability of automatic systems haunted me and with visions of broken barriers and shattered windscreens I prepared my file and passport as Aachen crept closer.

By 1995 Belgium, France, Luxemburg, West Germany and the Netherlands signed the Schengen Agreement, although it would take another two years before it became an integral part of the almost borderless EU. It was a great step forward but no one had seen fit to tell me in the preceding 15 years and so, as Austin's wipers did their best to bat away the truck spray and rain, I travelled the last twenty miles of Belgium with a pensive expression and my passport clenched in my teeth. How far inside Germany I was before it dawned that the exits had become Ausfahrts I wouldn't like to admit, but in the thickening drizzle the Belgian Autosnelwegen slipped seamlessly into the Deutsch Autobahn and suddenly Austin and I were trundling along the world's fastest road.

Even with the full majesty of his 61 horsepower engine firing away, Austin was like a pedalo that had strayed into a powerboat race. Germany's car industry carries so much weight that successive governments have failed to cap the speed limits and as Austin and I hugged the slow lane Porsches and Audis tore past, little more than smudged blurs. Everyone had warned me we wouldn't be welcomed but around us trucks crawled past blocking out the watery light seemingly respectful of Austin's senescence. People shot past with supportive toots and thumbs up. The only group who drove dangerously close, blocked me in and generally went out of their way to terrorise, bully and threaten a fifty year old car doing his best, were, of course, trucks emblazoned with a single black F. All day long they would tailgate, veer dangerously in front of Austin and generally live up to their reputation as the world biggest arseholes.

The constant hulking truck vents behind had me wishing I had a speedo (or a gun, although a hammer or a crowbar would had done). Since its demise I had been attempting to calculate speed with simple maths. Speed equals distance divided by time if I remembered correctly and so, if the distance from this sign for a Raststätte service area was 25 km and it took me 30 minutes then I should be doing 50 kmph (31 mph). According to my reckoning that was exactly the speed we were doing, which was terribly slow even by Austin's standards of dotage. It seemed clouds were going past faster than that. No wonder the French were so upset, at this rate we could hope to be in Jordan before New Year.

As I attempted another sum and the French threatened to crash violently into Austin's backseat things took a very dangerous turn for the worse. Austin had been cheerfully leading Count Basie's Jumpin' at the Roadside, tapping his wipers in time with Sonny Payne's driven cadence, when he gave a minute sigh. His wipers slid to a halt and in an instant what little I had been able to see of the road in front disappeared behind a grey green blur as if I had crashed off the autobahn into an algae filled pond. Only the taillights of the Slovenian cattle truck in front suggested otherwise.

If I had been terrified before now panic fought for control as I struggled on through the cataracts of spray as the traffic roared and cracked and bleated around us. For an eternity we drove practically blind in an endless storm inhabited only by tumult and the wrestling aromas of fumes and the pungent forests outside. Austin shook and quivered with each passing vehicle and we cowered, trembling and petrified, trying to make it to shore.

At the next Raststätte the awful tea did nothing to settle the shaking. Nothing I did would persuade the wipers to return to life. I had tied my bootlaces to them in the vain hope that I could operate them manually through an open window. They wouldn't budge. If the weather and traffic continued then we were blind. It was little consolation that the same mechanics who built Austin were the ones who built the Lancaster bombers of Dambusters fame. Just fifty miles north of our forced halt, the bombardier of Squadron 617 yanked heavily on an Austin Motor Company lever and away skipped Wallis bouncing bombs across the water and into legend. We were hardly living up to such exalted history. Then again thirty years later the Austin Motor Company built the hideous Austin Maxi and ruined everything.

We sulked for an hour. I chewed on a dry Fig Newton. It didn't help so Austin, rattling with his collection of mysterious ailments, and I, with my chest and burning throat, pulled dangerously back out onto the Autobahn in search of the next campsite.

On top everything else that day it looked as if we had lost not only the original campsite but possibly a town too.

According to the diary they had stayed at 'Rottzbitz' on the far side of Cologne. It wasn't in the guidebooks, or on my map. A Google search before I left had only given me the option to look at Ritz Crackers Ritz Bitz near Exeter, UK. Even the presence of a lake wasn't enough of a clue. Perhaps it had been lost beneath progressive tsunamis of post-war development. Cologne, in particular, had been levelled by the Allies and had only just really got going by the time my parents sauntered this way. But surely we couldn't have lost an entire town and lake? 'Don't know, son. It was just a brief stop. Austria was the real goal. Maybe your mum had too much sun or sauerkraut.'

Making it to a safe haven wasn't my biggest worry. Above all I feared that if I took Austin to a German mechanic without the MOT papers and proof of his road-worthiness that some old curmudgeon might reel off a list of rules and ground us permanently.

Tired, sore and coughing as I was, I was aware that I might not be thinking entirely logically, as evidenced by the vile tea I was still attempting to drink, so I asked Austin. 'What do you think, mate? Shall we push on to Cologne when the rain slackens and take the risk? Surely the weather has got to change soon, it's been raining all bloody week now.' Austin refused to comment and so, fearing more for an end of the trip than life and limb, I made the questionable decision to climb back in and turn the ignition key.

Germany spent the rest of the day as a glaucous mystery as we slipped treacherously into the Rhine Valley. Thankfully, after three terrifying hours we caught a glimpse of the sign for Köln sud. With a relieved exhalation we took the A555 to Bonn and, with the Roden Kirchen Ausfahrt, began searching for our campsite amongst the suburbs of Cologne/Köln.

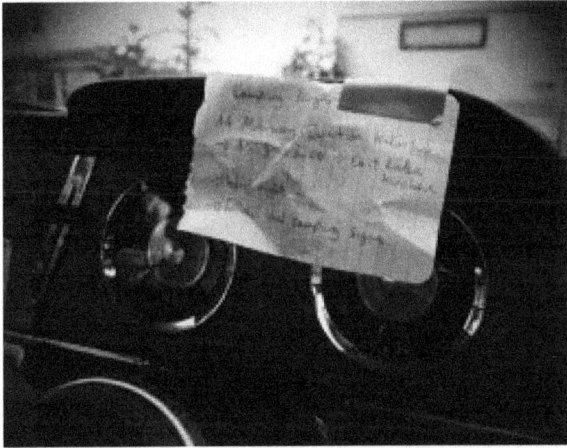

The site was selected from the British camping guide in the hope that there might be some like-minded people hunkering down beneath their canvas. There wasn't. There would be no jovial Dutch to cheer me on or young adventurers buzzing with the joys of travel. What I found on the banks of the Rhine was the antithesis to exploration and romance. After a week's travelling I had begun to believe that the position held during my parents' day had been usurped by the backpacker hostel. My parents had fled the suffocation of their lives and, as they hammered in tent pegs and rehydrated cabbage, they were invited for dessert or a beer with Dutch and Swedes who had fled the shackles of their own confinements. Beneath the dripping trees, with the Rhine moving slowly south I had found not a place of adventure but one of retirement. Maybe this is where the Sixties romance went, it didn't evaporate or die it simply grew old and became a creature of habit. It didn't want new friends, new experiences or new challenges, it wanted a TV, a microwave and oversized novelty flags. It wanted a catalogue of rules and instructions, to know where to park, walk, and breathe. It now brought lawnmowers and strimmers and the crap of home on holiday. Four campsites into my venture and what I found were lifeless husks, retirement homes with aluminium walls and butane lunches. I couldn't imagine anyone hauling themselves off their €5 plastic garden furniture to introduce themselves.

It was probably against the rules.

'You still have tonsils! Why?'

It was difficult to answer with the tongue depressor in my mouth.

'They should be gone in an adult. In Germany no adults have them.'

'E ownee 'oose 'em iv oo ave 'onalius.' I wasn't going to attempt 'tonsillectomy' without the use of my tongue.

The professional young doctor was built like a rugby player. 'With some antibiotic we cure up the infection which is causing the cough. There is nothing wrong with your lungs.' The news that I wasn't about to die of bronchitis cheered me up no end. 'But you really should have those tonsils out. In an adult they act as a sponge for all manner of bacterial infections. It's only a matter of time before it gets infected again. The bacteria just sits in them breeding and getting worse. It is not very nice. Very yuck! Well it was nice meeting you, Herr Button. Good luck with your trip and don't forget to get some new shoes.' As we waited in the chemist's downstairs I felt I had to clear something up. 'Does he think I'm walking all the way to Jordan?' My friend Klaudia looked a little confused, 'Possibly' was all she was willing to risk. After a day's walking along the Rhine I had somehow added a sprained ankle to the list of troubles and driving from Köln to Offenbach had been incredibly painful. Each time I dipped the heavy clutch a stabbing pain would flash through my ankle making me snarl and hiss. Continuing the journey in just first gear was not one to be entertained and so instead of stopping in Frankfurt Au Main as planned I had called an old photographer friend who lived in the next city, Offenbach.

Klaudia had offered me a place to stay at her mum's home while I dragged my sorry hide to the doctor's. The surgery staff had been friendly and polite, even allowing me to skip ahead of the queue, which showed a strange reparation from my parent's trip. My dad's dislike of Germany was based not on animosity towards the Axis shared by some of the British; after all, as the war broke out he was a child and the combination of no school, endless bombsite playgrounds and a little innocent looting meant a rascal-ish enjoyment that only a five year old could get away with. However, while Jimmy had been buying bratwurst a local tried to push in. For a country full of rules this was too much to bear and the queue-criminal was offered a 'thick ear' and a stern thumbing indicated the back. He was still a little annoyed after standing around exchanging Belgian francs for Deutschmarks in a back alley. This had also seemed wrong in civilised and ordered Germany.

The modern euro was one of the few luxuries I had on my side. I didn't have to carry stacks of notes and find crooked men in shady alleys to exchange money. The euro would take me through Belgium, Germany, Austria and Slovenia. It would be possible to get through Croatia, Serbia and Greece and as far as Asia Minor. It was one less thing to worry about. Although the way the euro crisis was developing I may well need more than just drachma on the way back.

Like the lifting of the borders, a single currency had profound physiological effects on unifying Europeans. Although first suggested as far back as 1929 by the League of Nations it wasn't until December 31, 2001 that the Belgians, Germans and Austrians ordered their last rounds with francs, marks and schillings. As dawn broke on the revellers the euro made its grand entrance after nearly three-quarters of a century. Although in the post-colonial world of Europe there is an irony that the first item purchased with euros, according to CNN, was a kilo of lychees, not in the markets of Paris or Berlin but off the coast of Africa in the tiny French overseas department of Reunion Island, but I'd like to think that the first thing purchased in Europe was a Danish beer, a croissant or a pair of lederhosen. Three million people from twelve European counties have a singular currency, but whether that number would increase or decrease by the end of the trip was probably up to the German Chancellor Angela Merkel.

Just days before the EU regulator had gone through the books and the Guardian had reported that five Spanish, one Greek and two Austrian banks had failed the stress test while another seven Spanish, two German, two Greek and two Portuguese had barely scraped through. This only worsened the confidence in the euro and although Merkel and Sarkozy publically stated that they wouldn't allow the Eurozone to collapse the British bookmakers Ladbrokes were happy to take bets on Greece defaulting. Merkel had her hands full preventing the wobbling Greek domino from toppling.

Jan's short history of Brussels' role in the EU had gone a little over my head and I thought a trip to the home of the euro and the Eurotower, where the Central

European Bank was situated, might offer some clarity, but after the doctor's we first went to Klaudia's father for lunch.

'The Eurotower is just an office block and the new place is still a building site,' said Klaudia as she placed a platter on the table. 'This one is the local one Frankfurter Rindswurst, that sausage is a Nuernberger, like the city, and that's Aufschnitt, Rohwurst, Gelbwurst Topfwurst and Fleischkäse Weisswurst. Papa, I don't think he needs to know all of them.'

We were sat in the sunshine amongst a charmingly ramshackle cacophony of summer flowers and fruit trees of her father's Schrebergarten. For the first time in what felt like eternity I had taken off my coat. With my foot on ice, antibiotics in my system and a table bowing under the weight of lunch the world was divine. I could hobble about a business district looking at building sites or I could rest my foot and spend the afternoon in lovely company devouring food that hadn't come from the Sixties.

'Schrebergarten means 'allotment' in English. This is a local cheese called Handkäs mit Musik and these are Allgäuer Bergkäse, Edamer, Backsteiner, Butterkäse. Brigitte is just bringing the bread. But young people don't like them. They think they are for stuffy old people. The Schrebergarten not the cheeses.'

These wonderful little gardens have their roots in the 17th century Schreber Movement, named eponymously after one Daniel Gottlob Moritz Schreber. Schreber was a passionate advocate of healthy living, and in particular the benefits of fresh air and the countryside, on child development. Through his People's Health, Volksgesundheit, he hoped to improve the lives of all Germans. Part of this included his Systemic Remedial Exercises, which he developed in an attempt to stamp out that adolescents' pastime of masturbation. He even went as far as to patent a host of exercise machines that resembled the bastard child of a home gym and a loom. With these contraptions boys and young men were encouraged to work off their youthful exuberance by vigorously pulling and pushing handles and levers in the sort of action that would normally only be reserved for the privacy of the hobbyist's own bedroom. With Schreber's device the average enthusiast risked finding himself reaching Olympian levels of forearm strength and stamina that put them in danger of lethal friction burns or possible sparks.

The machines disappeared but the gardens flourished and throughout Germany's history, during the rough times, the Schrebergarten supplied solace, escape and often the only source of fresh vitamins. Today they have generally mellowed into community gardens where, for a monthly rent, residents can escape their apartments and shelter amongst the sunflowers and sweet peas in the sunshine. Klaudia's papa and his partner, Brigitte, still grew masses of fruit and veg between night shifts at a taxi company, but many gardens have settled into formal right angles of strictly manicured lawns and picket fences. 'Bread? This is Bauernbrot, Doppelweck and this one Sesambrötchen. People aren't supposed to live in them but a lot just want to get away from the city in the heat and only go home when they need some central heating. The organisations go mental if they catch you.'

In a world of petty tyranny the heady power of these councils is a German cliché. Some have strict rules on what flowers may be grown, the length of lawns, even how they are decorated. Although, I noted, that by some miracle of kitsch, gnomes have survived to identify like-minded individuals in that 'Here lives a serial killer'. A cheerful plaster beardy-weirdy lets others know 'My patio foundations are full, find your own shallow grave!' I believe it is a bit like swingers and pampas.

'Papa says it will only take you a few hours to drive to Kuftstein in the morning. There are no borders like when he came here.'

At the same time as my parents trundled east, millions of Yugoslavs, Tunisians, Greeks and Moroccans were heading for better lives as Gastarbeiter, guest workers, in West Germany. Klaudia's parents had simply stayed. I picked up the fork keenly as Brigitte sweetly began to load up my plate and Papa sleepily batted away obdurate wasps.

'She says help yourself to the rest. There is caviar, fruit, pickles, salad cucumber, and mangos, boiled eggs, Löwensenf mustard, boiled Salzkartoffeln potatoes.'

We talked lazily through the hot afternoon. Amongst the flowers and in the company of a family, thoughts turned to home and I realised for the first time just how deeply lonely I had been. The hours of driving were exhausting. I missed Nicole, our garden and our bantams. I wanted to sit amongst our sweet peas, our spinach and under our sun. My goal seemed so far away.

Klaudia's father offered me a beer as his Macedonian flag flew in an unfelt breeze. He seemed very unimpressed with my whole plan. Having left decades ago he wasn't very keen to return. 'There is nothing there, we have some family and we occasionally go for a holiday, but it is a dangerous place. And it gets worse with all this euro problems. Yugoslavia is still an angry place.' His flag snapped above the flowers, a great sulphur sun against a blood red sky. Then it collapsed.

'He says we have some family there that you can maybe stay with them if you aren't murdered. Brigitte's is asking if you'd like some dessert?'

'What?'

'Dessert? Brigitte has got cheesecake…'

'No, the other bit.'

'He thinks you'll get murdered in your tent, probably in Macedonia.'

Chapter Seven – Weather Bird Rag
(Louis Armstrong)

Wednesday 12th July 1967. Kufstein/Austria
After lunch we began to make our way down, it was here that the fixed ropes were needed. Coming across the snow we saw another Chamois this time, it didn't run away. By the time I got to the hut I was completely shattered. We stopped for a litre of wine to celebrate the days work but poor old Jim had to drink it nearly all himself, neither Pat nor I liked it.
Mileage for the day 184   Acc. Mileage 767

They were famished. Their last blamanche wobbled in places but generally oozed as Pam brought it over. The table was littered with the debris of dinner. They had spent nearly a week commuting between the peaks and the valleys and now they could hardly move. Scheffeur had just about finished them off.

The trio had devoured oxtail soup, Fray Bentos steak pie with fresh potatoes and beans and were still ravenous. And sore. Very sore in places, but Pam couldn't think of anywhere else they would dream of being. A moment's distraction and the ugly pink dessert nearly escaped into Pat's lap.

They had dragged their leather boots, heavy thermals, nylon windcheaters and canvas packs across the continent, hundreds of miles from the King's Road, only to leave them in the tent as they clambered through the sunshine in shorts and t-shirts. No longer weighed down by the damp layers of Scottish wool they needed at home they felt as fit, bronzed and lithe as the chamois that dance effortlessly across the Tyrolean scree.

On the table amongst the dirty cups and crockery were the postcards for Ernest and Jeff. Two colourful tokens full of boasts and glories from the day's ventures into the Alps. They had speculated whether it would change anyone's mind back home. Draw them out of the Little Englands and Little Wales towards the soaring magnificence above the camp. 'Can't imagine Ern with Wurstsuppe?' said Jim stretching like a leopard. 'Sausage in a soup! Sausage? Soup?' They knew they were picking on Ern but he seemed to embody all those who stayed behind. With each passing day they thought less of home as they slipped blissfully into their own dream. With each mouthful of corned beef they severed a thread on the anchor grounded in Portland Rise. With each worzel soup, each Applesaft, each wurst they remade themselves, neo-lotus-eaters.

Scheffeur blushed in the dying light. Pat saluted the peak with his spoonful of blamanche.

☞

The first fingers of the early light began to caress the valley sides. As I sat with my feet in its biting glacial water the brook emerged from the damp firs and traced the edge of the meadow before falling gently away into the roiling mess of the Weissache. There it thrashed about in the torrent, through, over and around boulders and logs, over and over again, eventually clearing the dark woods and rushing angrily into the unhurried River Inn. Disciplined by the superior strength, it curved away beneath the battlements of Festung Kufstein where the day before, after an exhausting ten-hour drive from Germany, I stopped a very nice young couple, disappointingly not dressed in lederhosen. 'Yah, I think it used to be right here, but there is a hospital here now.' They indicated the hospital as supportive evidence. Campsite number four lost to the vagaries of development.

The tourist office, in the medieval heart of Kufstein, had phoned ahead for me and eventually I found a campsite on the edge of town and settled in.

Awaking in the next morning I replaced the frozen peas I had used to sooth my ankle with the delights of the alpine brook. The coldness felt great. I ate a breakfast of muesli and celebrated local blueberries from my canteen. I wasn't sure if I was supposed to freeze my foot in the morning too, but I let them go numb and lay back in the meadow flowers pondering my situation.

My parents had come here to climb and walk. Over the weeks the trio had gelled into a gentle syncopation that, along with the warmth of the summer, had washed away their frenetic home life and left a polished stillness and joy. Jim was still keen to begin mountaineering; after all, he had dreamt of little else during his hated apprenticeship. The original plan was to climb the highest peak in each nation, but why climb in the monotonous flatness of Belgium? Ben Nevis was twice as high as le Signal de Botrange. Why pause long in West Germany when the Austrian Alps were just over the border?

I had planned to repeat some of their walks and climbs. They seemed easy enough; I'd done a few in New Zealand and Japan, there had been a few years of cheerful bouldering sessions while at university in Staffordshire but I hadn't really discovered their love of climbing. Possibly it was too much kit, too much commitment or simply too much plummeting but neither my brother nor I have the sort of head for heights you would think we should as the children of mountain lovers.

So I thought I would spend a few days gently hiking through the charming Walleralm pastures around Kufstein and see where it I took me. The realisation that any further damage to my ankle could stall the journey was a sobering consideration, so I planned to wander slowly up to the Hintersteiner-See Lake, sat majestically above, and possibly prove my manhood by having a refreshing dip in the glacial waters.

Taking my foot out of the stream I pulled on my new shoes. They may have been über-cool fell running trainers but to me they would carry the shame of being my first orthopaedic footwear.

Under a blistering sun my first start wasn't the heroic success I'd hoped for. Following the trail map I had negotiated a tricky corner when a bread truck, hurtling around the bend, sent me diving over the barrier into a thicket of brambles. Spitefully they clawed and bit me until I finally extracted myself and retrieved my shoe. I looked like I'd been in a bear pit all morning. Retreating, I glimpsed an old lady, bent almost double with age and her shopping, taking a path I had mistaken for a goat track. The gravel path led slowly past beautiful alpine cottages with firewood stacked under their eaves and balconies bursting with geraniums and trailing lobelia. It's all to easy to mock the kitsch and cliché but on a bright morning as the wood warblers called and the grass hummed with crickets and hoverflies they cheered me up and seemed perfect beyond words.

Passing through the meadow the path petered out into a track and lifted into the dark wooded hills above. The trail promised that once entering the trees the world of valleys and meadows would remain hidden until one surfaced in the Wilderkaiser range miles above. At the whitewashed Locherer Chapel I washed my face in the icy mountain spring as centuries of pilgrims, warriors and now hikers had done. In the glades, lesser redpolls chased away willow tits in noisy challenges. I perched in the doorway of the 1739 chapel, built to celebrate the War of the Spanish Succession, and looked back the way I had come. Framed by dark firs and spruce the meadow swept away in a long slow arc rising up through the gap into a towering green wave feathered with pale scree and the bones of the Alps themselves. I had no map and no real need to know where I was going; it was enough to be dry, clean and hobbling through the sublime beauty of the Austrian Alps, beneath a lapis sky.

Before I had left Cornwall, a friend, Sam, had taken me aside in the pub and said, 'Make sure you stop and take things in. It's going to be a hard, stressful and exhausting journey. If you don't take a moment here and there to just enjoy it the trip will simply be an exercise in purgatory.'

From the very start the plan had been to travel hard for two or three days, to cover some distance and rest for a day in between. This regime was imposed simply by the refined speeds Austin travelled at. We would bundle along in comparatively crazy time like the triple pace trumpet of Miles Davis's Birth of Cool following the surge with a long drawn out note, a pause for breath and to absorb and appreciate and drink in the moment.

To encourage me to stop and take a break, as much for my ankle's sake as my mind's, I had taken along my journal rather than simply my notepad. As I chomped away at an apple I was inspired by a meeting with Kurt, an Norwegian octogenarian who had cycled from his home in Bergen. He had the finest moustache I had ever seen not carved on a Victorian war hero and had often bivouacked in fields and forests as he pedalled across Norway, Sweden, Denmark and Germany bound for Reggio Calabria in Italy. He'd recently lost his wife to Parkinson's and the long hard days of cycling helped numb the pain.

I would write a letter home to Nic; the old sort that takes days and waffles and ambles, taking pleasure in the serendipity and chaos of a wandering mind.

As I scribbled the first few paragraphs, failing to express truly the beauty of the valley, heavy with its melange of damp earth, pine and cattle, something Kurt said came back to me. 'If you were a positive person then you had travelled a quarter of the way already.'

If you were pessimistic, then you might want to argue that in reality it was actually an eighth of the way, as I still had to come back. You might want to allude to the fact that neither Austin nor I were in great shape. Or point out that Syrian tanks now fired upon unarmed protesters in Hama and, more worryingly, the EU had begun to impose sanctions against the Assad regime.

At some point I was going to have to address alternatives to crossing into Syria, but I wasn't going to focus on that today. Today would be full of warm, fuzzy memories of ski trips with their associated strudel, schnapps and C & A salopettes. Later I may celebrate this milestone with a creamy Einspänner coffee and a Kaiserschmarrn pancake smothered in plum jam, but this morning while the sun was out I planned to follow the vague signs promising the Gaisgraben Wasserfall and eventually the Hintersteiner See nestled above.

For an hour or so I peacefully placed one orthopaedic foot in front of the other, enjoying the simplicity of the movement. No gear changes, no fuel worries or map reading. Just rolling those feet, heel-roll-toes-lift, repeating the doctor's advice a thousand times as I tramped beneath pines still dripping from last night's storms. With the slow skiffle of tread against gravel, a lazy brushed snare to a gentle backbeat of yesterday's raindrops, my mind wandered back to my family. I find an infective rhythm in movement, one that tainted me early. I simply cannot sit still. My brother, so similar that people assume we are twins, was spared this blessing, or curse; instead he was gifted with Mum's love of music. My movements are to the beat of horses, pistons or feet against a path. Rob, a drummer, a pianist and a DJ, taps, brushes and hammers out his own tempo. While I'm confined to my own limited cadence, he craves and creates, even conjuring, seemingly to me, like a magician – no, rather an alchemist – rhythms and beats for thousands to enjoy and follow. Both soloists in our own way, we're seemingly so different in thinking. We both find a pulse, a cadence and rhythm from the different corners of our parents' life as their love of music and travel winds its way throughout our souls.

The world of brooding firs and pungent mosses opens suddenly and I'm blinking in the sunlight, squinting back down the valley, over sleepy cattle and their pens to the campsite barely visible in the belly of the valley. I take a seat beneath a wayside crucifix with its votive hornbeam and continue my letter to Nic. My moods are mercurial. Kurt and Austria have stirred up a lot but as memories of my family swim about my mind there is still that victory: a quarter of the way. A pair of golden eagles spiral in the thermals between the peaks. They hang above the Kaisergebirge then wheel away towards Saint Johann in Tirol and Zell am See, my last stop before I cross into the unknown of Slovenia and the Balkans.

Only the previous year, when Liechtenstein joined the Schengen Agreement, Austria lost the last of her borders. Today you can leave, in any direction, without showing your papers. When the original crew arrived at Zell am See their passports were filling with stamps in heavy ink. In 1967, Austria, still bowed from the shame of the Second World War, found itself pushed hard up against Churchill's 'Iron Curtain', which stretched 'From Stettin in the Baltic to Trieste in the Adriatic'. A large ripple draped itself around Austria.

To the south it was Tito's Socialist Federal Republic of Yugoslavia. The east was controlled by The People's Republic of Hungary and the northeast by the bipolar Czechoslovak Socialist Republic. Pushed hard up against the oxbow of communism the decision to remain neutral after the Allied occupation seemed a prescient one. Just six months later Czechoslovak's première Alexander Dubček attempted a degree of liberations that took him too far from Moscow's sanctioned directives. Dubček's Prague Spring brought down the wrath of the bombastic Khrushchev. Tanks and troops of the Warsaw Pact violently crushed the protests and Dubček was removed from office. It was a brutal lesson to everyone behind the Iron Curtain, but the neighbours heard every blow and winced powerlessly.

Austria, along with neutral Finland, Sweden and Switzerland, chose to remain outside the EU because of its alignment with NATO, but with the fall of the Berlin Wall and the subsequent dissolving of the Warsaw Pact the nearest Russian tanks were thousands of miles away, safely on the far side of both Hungary and the Ukraine. In 1995 Austria and the others became full members and borders began to evaporate.

A quarter of the way there. Kurt had given me a sense of scale and the litany of aches and pains, mechanical and muscular seemed only challenges not barriers and now suddenly I could in my mind see Lake Bled, the Parthenon and glorious Istanbul.

A single raindrop dragged my attention back to the real world. So engrossed in the birds and the future I hadn't noticed the world had changed. The droplet was a warning shot of the bruised and angry storm that crawled over the peaks from the south. The valley walls formed an embouchure and through it a single roiling thunderclap, a darkly sonorous note that shook the Wilderkaiser.

More warning shots thudded around me as I made a dash for the Gaisgraben Wasserfall. There was no chance of making it to the Hintersteiner-See before the storm arrived so having been disappointed by the woeful trickle of the waterfall I dashed back as quickly as my ankle would allow hoping to get back to the campsite before the first downpours arrived. I must have made the right decision because as I passed a cottage the aproned women on the doorstep scowled at me and with a chain of Deutsch, shooed me towards the valley yelling 'Dummkopf' after me.

As if my presence were a brutal source of annoyance, a horse fly bit on the testicles of Austria, the skies darkened and I suddenly found myself kicked and punched by very angry meteorology. No weather has ever hated anyone more in history and the thunder and lightning stamped the valleys as I fled the storm as if pursued by Frankenstein's monster. Shambling into the campsite I threw myself into my tent with a little more theatricality than might have seemed necessary as a cannonade of rain hammered the site.

The integrity of my tent's promised waterproofing had been of some doubt for a few days now. A few suspicious wet patches had me a little concerned about incontinence but as the skies opened there were no doubts. The tent leaked like a sieve. Droplets formed under the dome and fell on to the netting where it pooled in favoured spots before massing enough weight to push through. The thunder hammered, ricocheting off the peaks and rolling like a boulder up the valley. The lightning lit the skies and I counted one thousand – two thousand – three thousand in an effort to calculate whether it was still advancing or retreating.

The anger with which the rain hammered the campsite was terrifying. As I huddled, the rain poured through my tent soaking my sleeping bag and pooling in the corners. With the conviction of a captain going down with his ship I fought gallantly to soak up the pools with dirty laundry while piling the clean stuff on high ground. Taking up my towel I fixed it through the loops above the poles so that it hung inverted, catching the majority of the raindrops forcing their way through the fabric. It held out valiantly for an hour but eventually it became so sodden that it began to drip through into the only dry place I had left. Abandoning ship I crawled onto Austin's back seat as night fell and as the familiar warmth of Austin's oil and leather cologne enshrouded me and I fell asleep with a single thought – a quarter of the way.

As the sky regained its temper the next morning I sheltered under the eaves of the toilet block and asked the owner in my best German, 'Regen stoppen?'

He was sorting the morning's recycling and paused and shrugged 'Vielleicht morgen'. Oh, great, that's not too bad I thought as he placed newspapers into the bin. The top one had an angry article about the possible sale of some local peaks. I wondered if the Austrians, like the Greeks, were considering selling their geography to relieve debt.

'Oder vielleicht September' wasn't the news I was hoping for. I put my own recycling in the bins and went to collect my bread rolls. Recycling was one of the things that had stuck in Dad's memory. 'I don't remember any street lighting, the stars were fantastic, but it was the first time we had even seen recycling. They were decades ahead.' Dad had liked the Austrians, he had found them quiet and polite. 'At that time they were still saying they had been dragged into war and hadn't really wanted to. But, they were really friendly and easy-going. Nothing was too much to ask. I liked them a lot. One day we stopped in this tiny restaurant for a snack. It turned out to be someone's living room! They made us coffee and pointed us in the right direction. Didn't bat an eyelid.'

I liked them a lot, too. They seem to embody the best aspects of German and Swiss efficiency without the rigidity and regimented coldness that the other two are often accused of. Yet the bread roll system confused me no end. The grandmother was in charge of roll orders and if you spoke nicely to her in the evening you could collect your fresh warm bread in the morning. Seemingly in her eighties she radiated life and managed the family, children and grandchildren alike, with the lightest hand. Yesterday I had opened my palm with assorted euro coins in it, She had select 40 cents and made a show of how much so I wouldn't be mistaken thereafter. Fresh to the country and with an addled brain, tonsillitis and painkillers I had no idea whether this was a bargain or a con. I offered her 80 cents for two and limped back off to my tent. I had only made it down the steps when I was hailed, 'Herr Button' as she returned 40 cents. Ducking under my washing line, straining under the weight of my whole wardrobe and the tent and groundsheet too, I opened the back to find three rolls. I was far too confused to return them so settled in for breakfast instead.

Each afternoon the brooding storms stalked the valleys like a drunken and abusive father. The weather forecast pinned to the notice board predicted a comparatively drier Zell am See. Kufstein had a row of five martial looking icons, slashed with lightning strikes, the sort special forces might use. I looked up at a grey, but otherwise dry, sky and decided to take a gamble. If there were no English speaking mechanics and I was going to risk the abysmal weather then it might as well be in the right direction. I packed my sodden belongings and chose to dash across the 1274m Pass Thrubstrasse for Zell am See. It would turn out to be a mistake.

The moment it was impossible to turn back the skies darkened and the traffic slowed in the appalling conditions. Through the rivulets coursing across the windscreen I was just about able to make out the taillights in front. We crawled through the Kaisergerbirge until we reached St Johann in Tirol, where I had first learnt to ski and where my mother, in her bid for middle-class-ness, committed horrible crimes against fashion in a lemon all-in-one ski suit. In the rosiness of my recollection Austria was all benign azure skies, pristine snow and handsomely stern people with solid Teutonic names such as Helga, Helmut and Heidi. In Jimmy's photos it was all Tyrolean sunshine and limpid streams coursing through the alpine meadows choked with wild flowers and lazy Austrian heifers. This wasn't how it was supposed to be. The original journey had seen blue skies while I enjoyed only a brief respite since Ramsgate. It was not supposed to be wetter than the Mariana Trench. By this point it was impossible to even see where to safely pull over. The only option was to follow the rear lights of the car in front.

Faster vehicles roared past, little more than grey blurs, and only the rocking of Austin's body gave them any physicality. Each time one of these ghosts shot past, the spray they liberated frosted my windscreen further and in the blindness, panic fought to gain control. What the hell was I doing here? Mum and Dad had swanned through the breathtaking passes, stopping only to pose as Jimmy snapped away at everything. They looked relaxed, content and at peace, not clinging terrified to a Bakelite steering wheel as half the world's rain coursed across the road.

I wanted to stop in St Johann but the signs passed before we were ready and suddenly before we had a moment to reminisce about ill-fitting ski boots, schnapps and jolly frozen noses we had committed to the Thrub Strasse and Memory Lane was left behind.

After several hours the rain became finer, the tessellated windscreen cleared a little, revealing a swirling opaque world, then suddenly we surfaced through the clouds and into a blinding world of sunshine. At the first chance I pulled into a viewing bay and turned Austin off and got out. Above the weather it was breathtaking. Austin steamed gently as I crossed to the barrier and peered down across the snowfield of clouds. Hidden beneath was the Hohe Tauern National Park. To the south the glimmering majesty of the Grossglockner tore through the cloud cover pointing the way south to Slovenian and the Balkans. To my back were the Kitzbühel Alps and below, through the breaches in the rainclouds, a ribbon of asphalt shadowed the Salzach River along the Zell Valley towards Kaprun. It seemed, glimpsed from here, so tantalisingly close.

This was the Austria my parents had come for, not for the House of Habsberg with its elegant empire and the urbanity of Vienna. It was the rural idyll of cowbells and cattle, of chocolates, of glorious green hills peppered with shy wildflowers and alabaster peaks punching up into the skies. And it was my Austria too, one of Julie Andrews flouncing about, warbling nonsense. When did a love of Fitzgerald, Coltrane and Cole dissolve into Do-Re-Mi and problems with Maria? Even to this day I would happily punch Christopher Plummer in the face for all those lost afternoons.

Still it was heart-achingly beautiful. The snatches of pastoral landscape unmistakably Tyrolean with its neat clutches of farms and barns, pellucid streams and meadows. Invisible storm fingers traced whorls through the grass and pulled the firs. Even up here, the silence was broken only by the bells of heifers and the distant keening of hawks as they scoured the tight slopes for marmots amongst the alpenrose. It was so beguiling, and Kaprun seemed so close, that I forgot the rain and set off again, heading east to Zell am See and our last stop before crossing the old Iron Curtain.

Austin is a gentleman of quite substantial weight. Even without my kit he weighed a regal 1.23 tons. Within minutes of our twisty descent I began to pick up hints of a nightmare. Once, when hitching through the Tien Shan Mountains of Kyrgyzstan the driver had swerved into a gravel bank, snatched my water and doused the pall escaping from his smoking brake pads. I never forgot the smell and although I was ready to use Austin's antiquated brakes sparingly and even though I selected a lower gear there was an odour of singed hair. It could only have been the brakes.

Turning the corner we descended terrifyingly through the cloud layer and into maelstrom again. I was fretting about the smell and concentration on the oncoming right hairpin so much so that I wasn't concerned about the slight left corner before it. It seemed inconsequential by comparison. In a heartbeat the friction was torn from my tyres. I snatched wildly at the steering wheel as we sheered off into a vicious sideways aquaplane. I felt the back wheels begin to join the front in a parallel glide toward the barrier and dark forest beyond. There was an instant to utter a 'Fuc…' before terror stole it away. As I whirled across the asphalt I was granted, in the expansion of time that comes with crystallising terror, a moment to lament my decision to chance it.

Nothing I could do made any difference. With a grace that was impossible to appreciate, we careered desperately towards the forest.

Then the offside tyres gripped savagely. Austin rocked and juddered with the bite. The original seatbelts showed no signs of being functional. I was thrown brutally at the steering column. Then the jolt woke them. The belt froze solid, yanking me violently back, my head missing the wheel by inches. The result was an equally violent wrench. It whipped my head back cracking it viciously against the doorframe and then the metal seatbelt buckle.

The blow gashed my head and very nearly popped my eyes out.

Adrenaline drove Austin the last few turns until we could pull over in a supermarket car park. With violently shaking hands I pulled the handbrake and turned off the engine. Miles Davis was silenced. My heart was beating so hard I thought it might seize. An oily dribble tickled my neck. Breathing short and shallow, I closed my eyes. Slowly, carefully I rested my forehead on the steering wheel.

Chapter Eight – Sippin' at Bells (Miles Davis)

Wednesday 19th July 1967 Bohinji/Yugoslavia
Boy what a night! It took me ages to get to sleep only
to be woken by a baby crying in the next tent. It must
have been somewhere around 3.15.am when it started.
I couldn't sleep so I got up, only to find that Jim was up
also. I made a cup of tea and we went and sat by the
lake. We sat there and watched the dawn break around
about 4.00am – it was really quite lovely.
Mileage for the day – nil. Acc Mileage 1032

*Since leaving the path and striking for the triple peak
they had climbed through the ether. It's a netherworld
populated only by a handful of ghostly shades that
greeted you with a guten abend, bonjour or a caio as
they passed. An Asphodel Meadows of the lost and
found. Pam massaged her feet and Pat poked his
blisters, waiting for Jim to return. Suddenly without
fanfare the curtain rolled back and below was the jade*

silver of Lake Bohinj. Further away across the green peaks was Lake Bled with its castle and island and grotty communist tourist tat. It was like bloody Blackpool. Politburo suits swaggering around with dolly birds buying crap. Trabants choke the streets with their blue fumes. And that god-awful dirge they called music. Yet it didn't look that bad from up here.

Pam lay back and staring at the sky watched a contrail sear through the heavens. Someone up there was rich and heading somewhere important. This was the first time any of them had been above the clouds and the plane and its travellers seemed to belittle their achievement. High above, seemingly days away, hung Triglav, splendid, regal Triglav. Jimmy had barely taken his eyes off it since they had arrived. He had been scanning for the first glimpse even as they handed over reams of documents, papers and dockets, which were scrutinised and tattooed with the correct seals. Before it was passed on to the next individual, who went through the same process before adding his own stamp and passing it on. An hour later, as it reached the last official in the row, he checked their . passport photographs in case they had changed in the last hour in the queue. Martial music played in the office and slogans and announcements filled the breaks. A portrait of Marshal Josip Broz Tito stared beneficently at a cobweb over the door. Thumped paperwork was scrutinised a final time and handed back, the initial docket rubberstamped and thrown in the bin by the last clerk and they were free to set off on the empty road to find their first communist campsite.

One of the most disconcerting things to see when you awake is the floor rippling. You are fairly sure that this doesn't happen, after all solid ground is supposed to be just that, solid. So sleepily you pat it again and a third time. Ripples flow out across the floor confirming that this isn't going to be a good start to the day.

Thick steel cables of rain had fallen all night and waking on my first morning in Slovenia I wasn't keen to find out why the integrity of my floor had altered. There was only one possible, unbearable reason. Carefully not to risk capsizing I unzipped the door and there in the vestibule was a small muddy lake with my ripples still escaping. I slumped.

The sun had just risen somewhere but it was apparent that if I wanted to keep my sleeping bag damp rather than sodden I had yet again to abandon ship and head for Lifeboat Austin. During the night the tent had become a sanctuary for other storm refugees; a colossal cricket, a spider and several unwieldy shield bugs hunkered beneath the canvas.

I was curled up on the backseat reading Nicolas Bouvier. As he passed through Yugoslavia he recorded in his The Way of the World 'By midday the brakes, our skulls and the engine were very hot'. My journey from Zell am See began and ended wetly but in the middle the magnificent heat hammered down gluing me to the leather seats. Austin wasn't ready for this inferno.

Idling in the Karavanški predor tunnel queue for forty-five minutes saw him overheat and stall over and over again. Either he needed restarting each time we needed to inch forward or else I had to tap the footbrake, dip the clutch, give a little rev and, until I grew an extra leg, use the handbrake.

We planned to take the Karavanški predor beneath the Karawanks range, then along the A2 for Ljubljana, turning left with the signs for Lake Bled. New and modern, the tunnel had only been open a month when it was caught up in the first days of Slovenian independence. The Ten Day War across June and July of 1991 saw concentrated fighting that involved the Serbian controlled Yugoslav air force and troops in helicopters attacking the Slovenes. Here, at least, there were no casualties.

It was a stressful hour of mechanical and mental anguish but eventually we were through and arrived with the rain at glorious Lake Bled.

Bouvier had moved on to gypsies and painting when there was a polite tapping on the misted window. With a squeak and a whinge the glass lowered to reveal a hatch of unruly hair and a smiling face.

'You look like a man who needs a coffee.' I was about to politely refuse when I realised I was exactly a man who needed a coffee. From the safety of his awning Mauel continued, 'We have a spare lifejacket too, if you want it,' nodding cheekily in the direction of my tent as it floated like a grotesque blue toad in a muddy pond.

Mauel's family were away hiking in the drenched Julian Alps with friends. He had stayed behind with his youngest, who slept in that mangled octopus way that only children can. The coffee was placed on the table and topped up with brandy. The canopy reached critical mass and a sluice of rainwater was swept off, very cunningly I thought, and into the washing up bowl next to a line of wellies in ascending sizes. The coffee steam spiralled lazily then was snatched away by the cold wind. I pulled up my collar and placed both hands round the cup.

They came here every year. It was a pleasant little campsite. They could drive here slowly from the Netherlands. They didn't go to Croatia any more. The Slovenians were lovely, the Croatians had forgotten visitors were more than the weight of their wallets. He shivered. 'Although the weather can be better.'

With Slovenia's succession from the Republic of Yugoslavia it was open to Europe's tourist keen on bargain vacations. Croatia, with its 1770 km of magnificent coast and over 4000 islands sold itself as the novo Italy or Greece. Slovenia nestled in the Julian Alps, named after Julius Caesar, and with only a toe in the Adriatic at the venetian gothic Piran followed the route of its neighbour and old owner, Austria, into the tourist market ski fields in the winter and hiking, kayaking and wild swimming in the summer. Slovenia made only minor changes and held back from the monstrous tourist developments elsewhere in Europe, with little or no changes, and today, twenty years after it gained independence, the tourist industry is worth millions of euros and employs one in ten Slovenes. A great deal of this is focused in and around the jewel in its crown the Triglav national park and Lake Bled.

Six months after the departure of the last Yugoslav soldier the newly independent nation of Slovenia was recognized by the EU and within the year the United Nations, too. It immediately applied for membership to the EU and was granted a full place on 1st May 2004 and started using the euro in 2007.

The coffee and brandy did their work magnificently and as Mauel brought me up to date on the world news I felt the tendrils of warmth spread through my torso. An hour later his bedraggled family returned looking as if they had been swimming rather than hiking and I made my excuses and returned to Austin.

Perhaps it was the company or maybe the warm rich coffee that put me in a good mood, I'm almost certain, however, that it was the several large brandies on an empty stomach that encouraged me to begin digging. Armed with Mauel's trowel I attempted to construct drainage channels that would alleviate my pond problems.

Fifteen minutes of digging did nothing. There are only so many times you can slip over in the mud before it becomes disheartening. I thought it was time for some breakfast so I found some dry-ish clothes and pulled on my waterproofs and headed out for the first of many walks around Lake Bled.

Nicole was sending me a parcel of every last piece of car paperwork she could find. I hoped that it would at least endow me with proof of Austin's health. In the meantime I would stalk happily through the pine-choked mountains that hemmed in the glacial lake. Pausing at some gap in the pines I would marvel again at the brooding Blejski grad castle glued to the cliffs soaring above the town.

On these long walks, cloistered beneath my waterproofs, rain crept in through collars and cuffs soaking my dry clothes underneath, but between moods the sun would force divine fingers through the clouds to rummage around the Julian Alps or gently caress the malachite lake.

How many times did I circumnavigate the shoreline? My mind wandered as my feet had little to do but avoid puddles and my eyes drank in the pines and castles. Who knows or cares? It was pleasant enough to wander with little to worry about for the day other than where to find some lunch. Sometimes I strolled, sometimes I strode. Other times I ambled, dawdled or traipsed around and around the water but I never tired of the Assumption of Mary Pilgrimage Church floating serenely on the morning mists or the alpine vistas beyond.

One afternoon I paused half way through a circuit for a rest and something to eat. With an apple and sandwich I picnicked beneath Vila Bled, formerly the summer residence of the Yugoslav royal family. War hero, benevolent dictator and president for life Marshal

Josip Broz Tito promptly appropriated it after he took power. Like all dictators he indulged in the delights of show trials, gulags and purges but was popular as a stabilising influence in the newly united Yugoslavia. As a key member of the Non-Alignment Movement he fostered good relations internationally and was courted and lauded by the West. He was also a hit with the ladies, marrying three times and raffishly unfaithful to the end of his days.

He used it to entertain guests or, rumour has it, lent it to his favourites for colourful orgies. Today it has been converted into a multi-star hotel but has retained its 1950 interior, promising French, Mediterranean and Slovenian cuisine and the opportunity to send emails from the Marshal's own desk. Although I think you have to supply your own orgy these days.

For an hour a day I lost myself in the ritual of maintenance. The bonnet was lifted and oil checked. The plugs were examined and Austin fired up. Oily rag in hand, I listened to the engine as the cylinders plunged up and down with the slickness of a Clifford Brown composition. Austin idled better and quieter than any car I have even known. He was beautiful to listen to yet on the way from Zell am See two more items were added to the litany of complaints. The oil indicator had been showing empty since Cologne even though I checked it every day while the temperature gauge claimed that after a ten-hour journey in 30 degrees heat Austin felt fine. You couldn't touch the bonnet without third degree burns but the dial registered cool. It seemed it too had never worked. At this rate I could look forward to arriving in the East pushing a single wheel along through the streets of Damascus and arrive in Aqaba with just a car air freshener and a steering wheel.

When not taking wet walks, nosing around the town or visiting the castles and churches, I experimented with tent architecture. The Tent Nappy, a towel hung inside from the pole loop, had found itself severely wanting, as it merely stalled the inevitable and then ultimately prolonged it. Surely the key had to be preventing the rain from breaking through in the first place and therefore a barrier was called for. The first attempt saw the use of my tartan picnic blanket, given to me, along with a beautiful wicker hamper, as a leaving present. I had laughed when I got it but thanked Jamie, Jane and Paula for thinking of it. Placing the blanket over the top created the Tent Toupee, which worked well until it came into conflict with the nemesis of all toupees – a light breeze. The tent had long ago warped from a place of sanctuary to one of torment. It was nearly two weeks since there had been a dry night's sleep and when Mauel's neighbour and hiking mate Leo offered me his gigantic tarpaulin, I accepted it gratefully. Entering the world of refugee chic my final design went by the grandiose title Tent-a-grad in honour of the castle above. And while it worked brilliantly the interior was so dark I couldn't tell day from night.

Feeling positive I purchased a new stove from a man hidden behind a rambling hedge of a beard. How I revelled in the simple joy of hot food or a cuppa whenever I wanted – such sublime freedom. I also rejoiced in the tumble driers. It took a few days to dry out my sleeping bag and all my equipment, which was safely stored in Austin. But above all I swam.

I swam almost everyday, regardless of the weather. Shielded by the vertiginous cliffs and forest slopes, barely a breeze troubled the emerald waters of Lake Bled. Tiptoeing across the few stones in spring heated waters in a drizzle or a downpour I would dive a long slow arc through the shallows feeling clean and free. The glide would bring me slowly to the surface where I paused taking in the beauty that haloed the lake and then, resting my sight on the Assumption of Mary Pilgrimage Church, I began to stroke slowly across refined mercury towards the bucolic little church on her isle.

Mum and Dad had swum. They swam in lakes, and pools and tarns. They stroked through inlets, bays and seas; other than making tea it seemed to have been their primary activity.

The lake was the perfect place to meditate and think problems through. With slow measured strokes you push fractionally closer. Occasionally another swimmer would pass with a simple nod and a cheerful 'Živjo' leaving only a ripple. Yet one afternoon, as a cloudburst pitted the glaucous surface Julia pulled up next to me and briefly became my swimming partner. I would only know Julia as an elderly head gliding across the lake sheathed in her old fashioned swimming cap, the sort that requires a chinstrap.

It soon became apparent that my Slovenian reached only as far as hello and having exhausted my repertoire we returned to English. 'My father used to work for Industrija Motornih Vozil. He was very proud to make your Austin cars. He loved that job. Even now the smell of car leather brings him back to me.' We breaststroked through water so clear and richly olive as to seem like melted glass.

'It is good that you do this,' Julia said. 'Children do not know their parents. They are a foreign country and a different time. I have been both. Maybe it is only when you are a parent that you hope your children will see you as more than just parents.'

Austria, and its memories of my early teens, had stirred things up. Along the way the young people of the diaries had grown and calcified into real people, young, fun individuals in an exciting time. Yet my passage through St Johann had whisked up all the recollections of my parents as I had seen them as a child about to become a teenager. The Pam of St Johann committed horrific crimes against fashion in a lemon ski suit and moonboots. Dad was equally embarrassing with the first strands of his comb-over and moustache that belonged in a previous decade. They were, of course, 'parents' and therefore authoritarian, old and square. Has any teenager ever seen their parents as anything other than dinosaurs? And these memories collided with the youngsters in the diary.

How could they be the same individuals who skied soooooo slowly and attempted to get my brother and I to get a haircut. When did someone who had owned a rare 1933 Hillman Aero Minx and sported a Chet Baker/Tony Curtis 'barnet' think that it would be acceptable to purchase a puce Austin Maxi let alone a Dacia Aro 10 Duster? 'That one was a bleeding disaster, too' Dad admitted later. For the first time since opening the diary months before, my parents were seemingly two separate entities again.

Julia's laughter tinkled across the lake and she lost her breathing for a moment. We trod water while she got it back and bells from the church rung out loudly. From the shore their sonorous note soothed as it echoed through the valley. This close it was almost abrasive, almost arrogant.

'The church is built on top of an old temple to our love goddess Živa. Couples go there to ring the bells for good luck. The man must carry a silent woman up all the stairs.' A skinny groom was hauling a chunky bride up the ninety-nine steps. He huffed and puffed, he staggered and rested. It was a scene as full of romance as a washing machine being delivered.

Regaining her composure we pushed on.

'You are looking at them wrong. One group is parents and one is children. They are not the same, but the same people. One is the, how do you say…ingredients, for the other. At least that is what I would want from my daughter to see.' It didn't make a lot of sense to me. The church steps were metres away now, the weeds inviting us in sweeping gestures in the wake of a wooden tourist Pletna.

Our conjugal deliveryman had reached the summit and as we turned back to shore, bridal dreams rang out across Lake Bled.

The trio and their Cambridge had made it into Yugoslavia because of Tito's bloody-mindedness. As early as 1948 he distanced himself from Stalin keeping the Soviets at arm's length, even going as far as to initiate the Non-Alignment Movement with Jawaharlal Nehru of India and Gamal Abdel Nasser of Egypt, two political giants of the twentieth century. But there are only so many snubs Moscow could or would take and very quickly the Marshal found himself isolated. In turn Tito reached out to the West. His reforms of 1963 saw the border restrictions slackened enough to let three tanned and overexcited Brits into the Yugoslavian Republic with the intention of scaling Triglav.

Triglav was, in 1967, Yugoslavia's highest peak but today, post-balkanisation, it finds itself the sole possession of an independent Slovenia republic. Since crossing the border a week before it had remained shyly veiled in summer storms but this morning the clouds pulled back and, squinting in the unaccustomed brightness, I gazed up at its beguiling triple peaks. So proud are the Slovenians of their mountain that it graces not just the national coat of arms but also the nation's flag as well. With the passing of Tito, his benevolent and uniting influence evaporated and eventually Slovenes and Croats pushed for independence. Due to proximity to the west and the fact that the republic had been territory of both the Austro-Hungarian empire and the Italians over the centuries, it was keen to distance itself from the ailing chaos that was festering in Belgrade.

You have to love a country who nicknames its violent struggle for independence as the Weekend War, Vikend Vojna. In fact it lasted ten days (the Desetdnevna Vojna) and had a reported sixty-six casualties but in the context of what was about to come, as the Balkans went up in flames, Slovenia had made a quick, clean and civilised exit from communism.

There was only one thing that I had to do in Slovenia before I left. One more pilgrimage. Mum and Dad hadn't stayed at Lake Bled under the communists; it wasn't to their liking, it was 'just like Blackpool' clogged with the blue smoke of Trabants, and party members buying up the limited tourist tat. They moved on down the road to Lake Bohinj nestled directly in the shadow of Triglav.

On their living room wall, paired with the photograph of them in Austria in 1967, was a second shot taken from the same trip. It showed the pair in swimsuits languidly wasting their day on a white beach beneath magnificent verdant mountains. Dad sipped juice from a camping cup, his Coppertone sun cream ready at hand. Mum sat legs crossed, head tilted in concentration, writing her journal. It was not, as most people thought, Greece but rather Lake Bohinj and the Alps.

Armed with a copy of the image I took a bike and

set off through the passes and meadows for Bohinj. I paused in the shade of haylofts half full in the summer and avoided beehives humming ominously. Unused to cycling it was a breathless 20 km of pedalling through the passes and alongside the river before I drew to a halt in front of St John the Baptist's church. With wobbly legs I got off and sat on the bridge watching the fish below in the gin clear waters.

My decision to hang on in Bled rather than come here to Bohinj hadn't been solely due to Mauel and everyone's hospitality or the weather. I had been waiting for my parcel to arrive. Having been pestered every morning for a week the very generous staff at the reception they brought it over the moment it arrived. Nic had searched high and low through the chaos that I call my files and had even braved the avalanche on my desk armed with a ball of string. The parcel contained a sweet letter and a pair of bags of beef Hula Hoops, but there was no MOT. I would have to continue without it and put my faith in bravado.

Thinking it would be simple to photo fit the mountains in Mum's photograph to those all around me I cycled slowly and leisurely around the lake. There seemed to be a German motor home rally going on and several tried to paste me to the hot road.

Eventually I reached the western end of the lake and found what may have been the campsite. I marched down through the pine needles and felt as if I were trespassing, which was exactly what I was doing. It was still very basic. Certain I had the right spot I strode to the beach through the dense pines confidently. But the mountains didn't fit this backdrop. It wasn't quite right, so I continued my search through the wooded shores looking for the exact spot. I stopped a girl working at one of the campsites and showed her the image. She just shrugged and said that there had been so much rain that most of the beaches were under water at the moment. My innocent investigations didn't go down well. Single men stepping out of the bushes with a camera are rarely welcomed on beaches, or anywhere for that matter.

At the first candidate I was scowled at by a father until I left. The next beach, a young lady was sunbathing topless as I crashed through the branches with my camera. Not sure who was most embarrassed, for a second I thought I should pretend to be the Modesty Police but withered under her glower. Anyway they probably don't have a Boobs Unit.

The next cove saw me lose my footing on the algae coated pebbles and, flailing wildly, disappear up to my waist in the lake. It was spiteful in its coldness, bitter beyond words. It was as if someone had plunged my genitals into liquid nitrogen without my permission. I gasped and groped for the shore where I lay beached, attempting to get my breath back and hoping my heart would start again. An Italian papa told his grandchildren not to worry about me and return to their fishing. Their canoe drifted out of sight as a swallow hurtled past obviously keen to tell his mates.

Lying back in the warmth of the Slovenian sun I considered my next move while I waited for my shoes to dry and for blood to shyly return to my lower extremities. The beloved Slovene poet France Prešeren may have written 'The lake of Bohinj calm in stillness lies, No sign of strife remains to outward sight' but I could no longer ignore the Syrian problem. The situation was deteriorating quickly and thousands of refugees were flooding across the Turkish border in the opposite direction I had been planning to take. The British Foreign Office was advising 'against all travel to the whole of Syria; British nationals in Syria should leave now by commercial means'. It was time to start looking for plan B. I ate my sandwich and Hula Hoops as I mulled over my increasingly desperate options.

My map lay drying and as it smouldered slightly it confirmed that Turkey had only two southern borders; Syria or Iraqi Kurdistan. The second route would involve driving the entire dusty length of Iraq and attempting to cross the border through eastern Jordan.

Against all common sense I checked the British Foreign Office webpage:

Iraq. – We advise against all travel to Baghdad and surrounding area, and to the provinces of Basra, Maysan, Al Anbar, Salah Ad Din, Diyala, Wasit, Babil, Ninawa and At-Tamim (At-Tamim is often referred to as 'Kirkuk Province').

I had begun investigating the possibility of heading south into Cyprus and using it to leapfrog into the Middle East just as Robert Byron had done when following his Road to Oxiana. There was a rumour of a car ferry to the island and then I could sail to Israel on a second ferry that may or may not be foot passage only. Once ashore in Haifa it would be simple enough to drive up through the lands of Abraham and pass through to Jordan at the Sea of Galilee and take the King's Highway south. The final possibility involved Alexandria or Port Said in Egypt and taking Austin through the blistering inferno of the Sinai on Route 33 to Eliat then to Aqaba perched on the Red Sea. The likelihood of getting Austin into either Israel or Egypt was unpromising.

There was a long way to go yet and as if the gods of authenticity had been invoked, Syria's borders would be sealed with blood once more. However, I would worry more about that when I got to Greece; after all I still had to get through Macedonia without being butchered in my tent.

Chapter Nine – The Party's Over
(Nat King Cole)

Tuesday 25th July 1967 Belgrade/Yugoslavia
We pulled into a Campsite just outside Skopje and to our astonishment there were no less than 8 busloads of British Students already there. We discovered that they were on their way to India, on a goodwill tour and they were all singing and dancing troupes from various regions of the British Isles. A group of students from the University of Skopje were supposed to come and watch them but they never turned up
Mileage for the day – 290   Acc Mileage 1709

In Zagreb Jim saw gremlins everywhere but there were gremlins everywhere. The secret police weren't as secret as you would have thought. Maybe that was the point.

None of them had experienced anything like it, even in the days of rationing and rebuilding. The proletariat shops were empty and the world muted. The cars and buses were painted khaki, then as they noticed this they noticed that the filthy buildings had been daubed with the same paint; a job lot from Dulux maybe. 'Can you imagine turning up and asking for the paint. How much, sir? Enough to paint a Balkan city please,' Pat joked darkly. The only colour came from the peppers. Twice as large as any apple they had ever seen. Deep red peppers everywhere. Stalls selling them sprouted up everywhere like blood clots on street corners and outside the empty shops. But it was peppers and only peppers that seemed abundant. Stopping in a clothes shop that sold only 1930s corsetry as the latest fashion, they furtively asked for cooking gas. Bemused but compliant they followed the directions up the stairs and entered a room where the hirsute man in a vest pointed them at the beds. Pat perched on one, Pam and Jimmy on the other.

'You did say "Cooking gas, gotvenje na gas", Pat?' asked Pam as she glanced about the dimly lit flat; the beds, a distressed dresser, its fourth foot replaced by a brick, and a bead curtain guarding the portal to worlds unknown.

'Yes,' he said with more confidence than he felt. Changing money and getting hold of the odd item on the black market wasn't unusual, but cooking gas seemed commonly available even in the countryside.

Jim and Pam busied themselves looking through the phrase book again, 'Pat, did you say...'

'Yes!' They were both absorbed when a woman parted the bead curtain. Pat looked at her in horror. 'Oh, fuck!'

Pam and Jim looked up from the book to stare at the vision in fishnets lounging in the doorway. It seemed that they had mistaken Pam for a young boy. Perhaps her mother had been right about the haircut after all.

115

Pat said 'I think we've ordered a prostitute by mistake!'

As Syria descended further into civil war the chances of scraping through and finishing Mum and Dad's journey decreased proportionally. With this in mind I chose to push on through Croatia, Serbia and Macedonia as quickly as possible. The original journey had breezed through anyway as the siren call of the Aegean drew them south.

I was sad to leave Bled. For the first time since setting out I was actually saying good-bye to fellow travellers rather than creeping away alone with the first light of dawn. The kids in the reception waved me off and Austin and I pulled away finally clean and dry and headed for Zagreb.

Croatia would seem to me the fulcrum of the East:West divide. Behind, the Alps and the efficacy of the West, in front, with each step along the A1 highway, more headscarves appeared on women, more onion domes on churches and more minarets pierced the sky as hawks circled above. Cyrillic rippled across the road signs as if the words melted in the Balkan sun. It really felt as if adventure was just around the corner. The sun pounded against British engineering as Chet Baker warbled his way through Let's Get Lost

'Let's get lost, lost on each other's arms

Let's get lost, let them send out alarms

And though they'll think us rather rude

Let's tell the world we're in a crazy mood'

The Slovenes had warned that the Croatians would be a nightmare at the border, insisting that I take everything out and allow them the opportunity to pilfer small items, but at the border they were politeness personified.

Dropping out of the Alps and into the Pannonian Basin the weather and scene flattened out. We had a frustrating two hours in Zagreb. A rereading of the journals reminded me that the others hadn't stopped overnight but rather pushed on to Belgrade in what is today Serbia. The city has undoubtedly changed since my parents' passage but Marshal Tito Square, Trg maraca Tita, is still hemmed in by the University of Zagreb and the Croatian national theatre. Still, Dad described it as '…a nothing. It was more like a big shabby town than a city'. Today, flooded with EU development money and tourist euros, Zagreb is a sprawling modern city replete with skyscrapers and chain restaurants. All I had to do was drive straight through the middle and on toward the East but it took two hot and frustrating hours to find my way out. Miles Davis was getting on my tits, as we struggled through the traffic, confused by the signs. Without movement Austin had no air-conditioning, which involved the opening of a window or the quarter lights. The sun hammered away at my patience and decision-making process. Another wrong turn. Then another.

By trial and error rather than anything else Austin and I were eventually spat out of Zagreb only to make a final and gargantuan mistake that had us following the road south towards the Adriatic coast. The signs read 'Karl vac and Rijeka' rather than 'Velika Gorica' and 'Ivanic Grad' as they should have if we'd been heading east to Serbia. It cost me an extra couple of tolls, which at the time was a burden almost beyond my wallet. Croatia may have applied for EU membership before Slovenia but a territorial dispute over the Gulf of Piran stalled their accession. Consequently Croatia would have to wait until 1st July 2013 to become the twenty-eighth member and therefore acquire the euro; as a result I was forced to stop and change money at a grotty services, hoping for an ATM.

The intense blue of the Croatian sky was reflected back from polished windows as I pulled in. It was a very hit and miss affair. Some stations glittered like beacons of modernity while others hunkered sullenly with troll-like ugliness. Neither sort guaranteed an ATM but at the former at least your disappointment was placated with cold bottles of water and polite staff.

If you stopped too long at these places, if you wanted to stare out at the world, hot and flat and blue and golden, and stretch your legs, gypsies, ragged and furtive, would materialise out of the bushes. Nicholas Bouvier sat with the gypsies of Yugoslavia while they played 'Crude, rousing, vociferous songs in the Romany tongue, which told of the ups and downs of ordinary life; poaching, small windfalls, the winter's moon and empty stomachs'.

These young men swaggered aggressively at me and demanded to wash Austin's windscreen knowing full well that the staff in the station had just done it for free. I came to believe that this was done simply to try to dissuade the gypsies from hanging around. If you were by some miracle able to prevent them then the headscarfed women, rolling hip to hip across the asphalt, thrust filthy children, all snot and sores, at you like some biological weapon.

It seemed strange and disconcerting to see such things in Europe. They appeared at almost every stop we paused at throughout both Croatia and Serbia. It was like something from a different age. These are neither the citizens of Bouvier's book nor the people of my grandmother. My grandmother, Little Nan, is believed to have been 'a gypsy from the East'. Yet the family has no real idea who she was because, until she stepped off the ferry in Davenport, 'Miss Davenport' did not exist. Who she was when she boarded in France we have no idea. She ended up in London on the arm of an Irishman by the name of Fred and together they would have thirteen children, eleven of whom survived. Little Nan's mysterious gypsy heritage gave the family a little romance and an excuse for my father's wanderlust. She may have been a whirl of vibrant colour dancing frantically through the torrid star filled nights of the East, who knows? But like so many others she fled before the darkness of fascism forced them out of the heartland. We were never to know who she really was but these people here in front of me, baking in the streets, knocking on my window attempting to stealthily wash Austin's windows, were not the gypsies of that image. These were the racist stereotypes of fear mongering bigots and I turned away from their appalling children with guilt and revulsion.

Almost surreally beautiful after weeks of mountains and forests the endless fields of stolid corncobs and wilting sunflowers stretched to a horizon populated only by buzzards and languid cranes. Occasionally the fields were punctuated by red tiled farms or squat towns forced to shimmy in the heat haze. We drove through blistering Croatia ticking off Velika Gorrica, Ivanic Grad, Novska, Nova Gradiska and Slavonski, each a good solid Slavic name. But there was little if any reference to these eastern towns in my guidebook. There seemed to be little to visit or marvel at this close to the Serbian border. Croatia is the new super-spot for vacations; cooler, younger and less developed than Italy to the west and Greece to the south. Its Dalmatian coastline is blessed with idyllic islets and turquoise seas, ancient cities and heroes like Marco Polo and Emperor Diocletian.

'That is the beautiful face of Croatia. The one everybody loves. She is beautiful and sexy. This here is the arsehole of Croatia. Nobody likes an arsehole.' I had to agree, yet after the sturm und drang of the Alps the opening of horizons above the Pannonian Basin felt both a relief and discomforting. There was a slight wooziness that accompanied the agoraphobia. The landscape simply flowed out in every direction like a desert or the ocean. A pelagic world without horizons; boundless and borderless. It was simply a sea of flower heads, sunflowers, with only the occasional farmhouse piling its way sedately home across the swells. Across a million tiny suns, each head a mimic of the one above. Yet together they rippled and moved, bobbed and bowed on the currents of the wind. Hamlets were islanded in the cadmium sea. The world above was blue as the ocean below it was golden; it all seemed twisted and upside down. The Yugoslavia of my parents was not one of beauty, but a mirror of the poverty they grew up in. The queues for rations, the fear of hunger, the grey lines and rules that kept all eyes turned down. The golden sea that Austin and I pushed through was not theirs. My parents' horizons had been Greece, Turkey and the Red Sea, but here in this baking world, away from the claustrophobia of the Alps, I felt liberated, I had finally achieved something. A near-death experience sharpened my focus. Out here there was no need to fret about windscreen wipers or aquaplanes, suddenly, in this world of a million tiny suns, the horizon opened its arms and my mind flooded out.

In the dead heat the cypress speared Austin with its stubby shade as I chatted to a collection of university students. Antun, the colour of teak after a summer off, offered me a cigarette and went on. He and his peers had little positive to say about the gypsies or his neighbours the Serbs.

The Slovenians had got off lightly in their secession but Croatia with its much larger Serb population would see five years of bitter and brutal fighting. The Serbs fought to stay within the Yugoslavian republic while the Croats wanted independence. There is an obvious irony that the type of nationalism the EU had been created to prevent after the Second War World was exactly what drove the wedge into the Yugoslavian heart, and ultimately brought about independence; 'Balkanisation' and inclusion in the EU. Accusations of war crimes, massacres and genocide were levelled at both sides. Families and towns were ripped apart in the struggle and this corner of the country had seen some of the worst crimes.

As we pushed on towards the border the pine shades fretted the highway. Belgrade was about an hour beyond the border and the border was about an hour away yet. When I nodded off at the wheel it was time to search for somewhere to pull over. As I searched for a road to pull off and settle down in the backseat I stumbled upon the Campsite Spačva, set back in the centuries old oak forest. Considering its proximity to the motorway it seemed a beautiful little place, but the camping grounds were closed for renovations explained the cleaner. She spoke good English while the receptionist spoke only Serbo-Croat. But they could put me up in a room in the hotel next door.

Later, after a shower, I sat in the hotel garden and watched tree creepers hop amongst the oaks. Above the Spačva River there was the flash of a kingfisher. Antun's stories of the area haunted me. When the dust had settled Serbia too had applied to join the EU. One major factor would be the bringing to trial of its war criminals. A week before I met Antun and his friends Serbia had caught the last one, a Croatian Serb by the name of Goran Hadžić. Hadžić was indicted on fourteen counts of war crimes and crimes against humanity. The BBC reported that he would stand trial for the persecution, extermination, imprisonment, torture and forcible transfer of thousands of Croats and other non-Serbs, on political, racial, and religious grounds. He was accused of massacres along the border. At Vukovar, Lovas, Dale and Erdut Serb paramilitaries forcibly expelled thousands of Croats and non-Serbs and killed hundreds of civilians and local police. Lovas was just ten miles away from where I sat eating dinner.

I went to bed with a very heavy heart.

I woke in the morning with the ghost of Eastern Slavonia in my head. It added a sense of foreboding as I paid my bill and went through the sacrament of departure checks. A Scottish couple who lived in Cyprus were in the car park. I can't remember if it was simply their accents, the fact that they were heading the same way or that I overheard them say something about Cyprus but I interrupted their conversation. They were driving all the way but unlike me had reached the border in a matter of days. The bad news was that there was no longer a car ferry to Israel and that the passenger ferry hadn't departed in months. The good news was that the car ferry from mainland Turkey still crossed to the Turkish control north of the island. It was something positive on such an ominous morning.

The border seemed only metres away but obviously it couldn't have been. The bereted guard smiled and demanded to see my Green Card, proof of third party insurance. I had paid a substantial amount of money for insurance to cover me in all the countries including Serbia. My insurance wasn't good enough and he pointed me in the direction of the office where I could, in the comfort of air conditioning, hand over fistfuls of Serbian dinar for something I already owned. I piled my mass of papers onto his desk and was building myself up to defend my corner more strongly when the officer decided he couldn't be arsed with this today and with that waved me across the border with a 'Goodbye, doviđenja!'

Pulling on to Serbian soil I realised I was about to enter with an antiquated car, no proof of roadworthiness and now no insurance, but looking at the other vehicles chugging across the boarder saw I wasn't alone.

I was keen to get as far across Serbia as possible in one day, but once across the border the road deteriorated alarmingly. The route I took south and east towards Macedonia was not very Austin friendly. Counter to what was stated in their 35p Yugoslavia Collins Holiday Guide – 'Motoring in Yugoslavia presents few problems' – the original trio had passed the time travelling to Belgrade counting road accidents. 'On our journey to Belgrade we counted five lorries which had turned over.' The guide also gave a beautiful glimpse into the Europe of the Sixties. 'Yugoslavia is a socialist federated state which is run by the League of Communists, but the nature of the regime need not worry the tourist in Yugoslavia any more than it does in Spain, France or Italy.'

My guidebooks had been an utter waste of money and I had only held on to them in case I was short of toilet paper.

The landscape became more impoverished heading east. The ruddy roofs of farmhouses bowed and twisted more painfully with every mile. Cars vanished and then tractors were replaced with donkeys and mules.

The landscape barely changed and it was only at each of the tollbooths that the eye had something that deviated from the fields of corn. At each the staff were friendly, smiley and often asked a few questions in stuttering English. How old? Money (cost)? And cleared me for the next section with a thumbs-up and a 'Good'.

The roads were pretty empty but in 1967 days could go by without seeing another car. Dad sat at the wheel playing his harmonica to keep him awake in the monotony and heat. There was nothing much to see as we passed through Lawrence Durrell's 'heartless dusty Serbian plains'. And with no air conditioning I opened the quarter lights and let in a tame sirocco.

Along the pitted roads there were countless no overtaking signs and an equal number of votive flowers left to indicate deaths. It seems no one reads the signs and as I began to near Niš I witnessed a grieving family mourning by the roadside where they put themselves in the very real danger of following their dearly departed into the next world with each rickety truck or overfilled Lada that passed.

It was about this time that I picked up two young hitchhikers at one toll. They sheltered in the shade of the booth, as I had seen so many do, and they proffered a thumb for a lift. It seemed like a way to experience a little more of Serbia than its endless heat hazed roads. They were heading to Niš and we chatted about university prospects and the universal language of football, but all too quickly their English reached its end and we fell into silence. At the next tollbooth they leaped out a little too quickly for me not to feel a little hurt that they planned to make a bid for a faster ride.

I didn't blame them because it would be after lunch when we finally reached Niš. But I could have done with their help, as the highway suddenly points you in the direction of Niš but takes you through a series of ever decreasing road works and turns until you are certain that this tiny road passing through the trees simply cannot be the main thoroughfare to one of the country's biggest and most ancient cities.

Confused, I pulled off into a car park. I had simply meant to turn around, but Austin, radiating heat like a boiler, was too large to swing around in one go so I was forced to pass through the gates of what turned out to be a breaker's yard of some description. I pulled up, opened the bonnet (as I did each time we stopped) and pulled out the map.

The crunching of gravel heralded the arrival of a giant. Dejan, dressed in a vest that may once have been green and was now stained with oil and grease, was flabbergasted that we had made it that far. His colleagues, wiry and furtive, wandered across the yard in ones and twos shielding their eyes and gawking in disbelief. I was invited to settle in the shade of their office porch and the table was loaded with tea and minutes later strangely feminine cakes and pastries. Dejan and the others rumbled away in Serbian and a smattering of English as tea was served and photographs for families went back and forth, some colour some monochrome but most on cell phones. I remember someone in Slovenia saying of the war in Yugoslavia 'you cannot tell how much blood a man has had on his hands once he has washed them'. But it is difficult to think of such things when a complete stranger offers you a large cream slice.

The Serbs are vilified as the new baddies in Hollywood and Europe. After all it was a Serb anarchist that plunged the world into the Great War with the assassination of Archduke Franz Ferdinand of Austria in retaliation for the annexation of Bosnia. They are seen by the world as the aggressors in the wars with Slovenia, Croatia, Bosnia and finally Kosovo. Yet they see themselves also as victims in the Balkan Wars. Atrocities were committed on all sides but the root of the aggression with which the Serbs attempted to control and carve out a Greater Serbia for themselves, and in particular their antagonism towards the Croats, lies deep within the Second World War. They were persecuted mercilessly by the pro-Nazi regime of Ante Pavelić. He is said to have collected over forty pounds of human eyes from murdered Serbs, Jews and gypsies. With the passing of Tito and the scrabble for power the Serb nationalists, in particular Slobodan Milošević, used the recent history to whip up the Serbs into a violent frenzy. The wars that spiralled out of control saw the involvement of NATO and even the UN. Today, Kosovo's departure from the union seems inevitable regardless of what Serbian nationalists want. Their only rebuke seemed to be limited to graffiting racist, and ultimately feeble, dictates the cubicles of service stations toilets.

Dejan had his apprentice, a whippet in oily rags, carefully wrap the remaining cake and offered it to me for the road. There were photos posed against Austin and we were united across nations and cultures with mild burns from the blistering bodywork.

Returning to the road I passed Niš and briefly struggled with the idea of stopping. As I did, amongst the Cyrillic the first signs for Thessaloniki appeared calling southward. Pushing on we left the arid farmland and passed through the Grdleicka gorge the site of one of NATO's major cock-ups in their bombing campaign. The Dutch airforce cluster bombed the town killing 55 civilians. The only good thing to come out of the event was that the Dutch refused to use cluster bombs ever again. Sadly no one else has.

The skies were starting to colour now but the ferocity of the sun had abated slightly. About 130km from the border, as the road began to coil up into the mountains that have hidden Macedonian and Serbian bandits and rebels for millennia, I pulled off into the Motel an Camping Predejane. It was a little jarring after a day of almost complete solitude. The large palace catered to all the needs of the traveller. It had several restaurants, a small supermarket and a hairdresser should I require one. From the terraces the elegant leggy blondes in fake designer glasses and tans lounged with practised nonchalance with mafia-looking chaps with white shirts and cigarettes. They didn't look like the sort who would stump through the dark earthy forest of wild boar and roe deer; instead they looked like they might be tempted with a little light sex trafficking.

There did seem to be thousands of visitors at the restaurant, but I was the only one pitching a tent. The site smelled of diesel fumes and a million belligerent bladders, but the view was pleasant enough. Peasants with hoes wandered home along the valley and, beyond them, over there in the smoky distance was the controversial Kosovo border. By the entrance to the car park a handful of handcarts rested with stubbly old men chatting. I bought a bag of peaches from one who said his sister was married to a computer engineer in Halifax. His smiley partner in crime sold kitchen knives and Christian iconography. Even to this day Mum raves about the peaches of Serbia. 'They were heavenly, just so juicy and the size of a child's head!' The other thing that she was obsessed with was swimming pools. They hadn't known at the time that the FINA World Championships in Aquatics had been offered to Belgrade. Although it wouldn't be until 1973 the country had gone pool mad. 'At the site we stayed at near Belgrade the pool was nearly as big as the site itself. And there was an ice rink. It is not every day that you can swim a few lengths of a magnificent pool, get out and while you dry in the sun watch ice skaters practise through the window.'

I had just set up in the car park and was boiling a

canteen of tea when a large Harley Davidson and a high powered Yamaha pulled up next to Austin. I thought that they would be German due to the bikes or Dutch from the friendly way they came straight over to talk, but instead they introduced themselves as Zarko and Polikarp from Skopje. Their English was faultless. They had stopped for a break on their way to a music festival in Serbia. Zarko, dressed in the leathers, jeans and cowboy boots acceptable for a Harley rider, went to double check with the receptionist that I should be camping on the verge. Other than Serb the receptionist had a few words of German, but the labourer in overhauls and sandals spoke perfect English to me between hefting a wheelbarrow of rubble into a skip.

The jocund Zarko returned with a beer for each of us as well as a burger. 'Serbia makes the best burgers. This is a Pljeskavica and the sauce is red pepper. It's called ajvar,' he said, handing it over. 'This place is famous for them.' The patty of ground lamb, pork and beef is seasoned and garnished. 'They even have their own festival for it down the valley there.' He pointed his Pljeskavica south. 'The Leskovac Grill Festival, or something like that.' We saluted the sunset and they remounted. Wishing each party a bon voyage they left me sat blissfully content in a Serbian car park drinking the last of my beer with peaches the size of a, very small, child's head for dessert.

What had seemed like whacky fun the evening before proved to be a very bad choice. I had thought it quirky to camp on the verge in a Serbian car park but the street lighting and the noise of the revellers staying at the hotel kept waking me up every few minutes . By three I gave up and slowly broke camp and set out to drive across Macedonia in a single day and, hopefully, crawl into Greece in the late lazy afternoon.

'There are no good campsites near Skopje so it's best to go straight through to Greece. Head for Kavala. It's got loads to chose from.' Zarko and Polikarp hadn't been disparaging about their homeland, only that the glories of the Aegean out competed them. 'Its never a hundred per cent safe to camp alone but Macedonians are just as likely to feed you to death too,' he laughed as he brandished his second Pljeskavica before they left the night before.

It was a beautiful smoky mountain morning. Ghostly tendrils reached around the valleys and explored the gullies. As we puttered through the mists there wasn't another vehicle to be seen in the distance or the rear view mirror. For a few hours this serenely verdant landscape was ours alone. Then suddenly, disappointingly, the world was full of people, vehicles and noise. There were hot and short tempered queues, feral dogs panting and prowling and a little street theatre piece entitled 'You can't just fucking push in pal, we've been here hours' with some collars grabbed and fists.

After an hour of this I was able to determine I was queuing in a queue for a queue to allow me to queue for the border. And when I finally arrived at the kiosk the Macedonians, unlike their Serbian neighbours, were having none of my shit about insurance and took my passport. There was a catechism, and beneath a desperately large Macedonian flag, they relieved me of fifty euros for fifteen days' insurance that I would only need for the four hours. The general belligerence of the staff made it very easy to decide to push on to Greece.

So for four hours Austin and I toured through a country of staggering beauty and an anthology of challenging potholes. Serbs and Greeks hurtled past keen to be in Greece (or the afterlife) as quickly as possible and as we tore round mountain passes and tunnels it was terrifyingly similar to the real life Wacky Races. If I had considered that Croatia and Serbia had a lot of crosses along their roadside then Macedonia is in a different league entirely. And it wasn't difficult to see why. At every corner, every bend, every straight, in fact anywhere it was possible to kill yourself in a fast and badly maintained vehicle, people tried to overtake. Slaloming down through the mountain passes cornering well and keeping ahead of the murderous trucks with the skills learnt under the tyranny of the Alps and the potholes of Serbia.

I paused to get my heart to slow after very nearly smearing Austin and myself along the limestone cliff wall and to let the queue behind pass. They all seemed very keen to have their own crosses on the roadside. I took a photograph of the little crucifix perched on the mountainside. A young Macedonian couple stopped too and I took their photograph for them complimenting them on their English. 'The young speak English and are positive, the olds only speak Russian and don't understand what there is to be happy about.'

Pushing on I stopped to use the awful toilets in the rest stop outside Tito Veles. They were awful, just a faeces smeared hole, with 'Kosovo are Serbia' and 'Macedonia isn't Greece' graffiti on the walls between faeces, and punctuated with neo-Nazi ciphers. Thankfully outside it said Athens 730km.

The Tito Veles of 1967 was 'the most outlandish place'. Macedonia has always lagged behind the rest of Yugoslavia and while 1930s corsetry was all the rage in Zagreb, the Tito Veles shops were empty. The whole place was painted khaki – the shops, the buses, even the cars. Their black Austin drove through the city to the spontaneous salutes of children and adults under some impression they were a one-car cavalcade.

Several hours later the driving had calmed as the passengers began to see their goal. They could practically smell the ouzo and olive oil. I stopped one last time in the Demir Kapija Gorge, the Iron Gates of Macedonia, the country's very own Thermopylae. The border was merely 15 miles away. High above, the naked limestone cliffs, white as bleached bones, were barely separated from the glare of the afternoon light, but down here it was cool. The River Vardar swept slowly past. Between the cars I could hear birds. It was a last pause before I crossed the half-way mark. Greece was more important than I thought. The unctuous Vandar River would guide me out of the Republic of Macedonia and on to the glittering Aegean beyond.

Their goal.

And now mine.

Chapter Ten – Elegie (Art Tatum)

Wednesday 26th July 1967 Skope/Yugoslavia
We had our dinner and then I had a shower, the water
was still hot – oh how civilised it felt; I thought I would
never get the dirt off. Jim and I then did the washing
up. We all three went and sat on the beach and listened
to the Greek music coming from the restaurant, and
watched the moon rise and looked at the stars. It was a
very beautiful evening and a wonderful feeling being in
Greece. I've yet to see the stars as they appear in the
Greek night sky. We sat there until 11:45, which was
quite late for us. Pat and I both felt that we had returned
home!!
Mileage for the day 260 Acc. Mileage 1971

The sheer colour of the world had been blinding. The
mournful khaki of Tito's property gave way after they
bought useless knickknacks so the Yugoslav guard
wouldn't simply take their remaining worthless dinar.

The notes had been the only colour in the entire country. Even that had given up.

The pageantry of Greece, the signs, the advertising, the smiles, the marching slippered and fustanella kilted evonse burst nova-like across the horizons at the border.

Pam marvelled at it as if surfacing from a dream.

It was like being let out of a cage.

Pat and Jim, both as golden as honey from the sun, were buying gas from 'Al Capone'. Jim had nicknamed him when they pulled happily into Platamon and it had stuck. Pam busied herself with the last of the camping stuff. They already had several cannonball-sized watermelons stacked against the table. In the years of rationing her mother had queued for three hours just so her daughter could try her first banana. She still felt guilty about how disappointing she thought it was. There had been a lot of firsts since then, first chips with mayonnaise, sauerkraut and sausage soup. Greece had already brought them their first aubergine, pomegranate and watermelons.

Placing the last of the cutlery on the table she lit another Senior Service, inhaled deeply and went to find Pat and Jim.

Pat held one inverted gas canister. Jimmy, in his freshly cut down jeans, held the siphoning tube while Al Capone held the empty canister. Al encouraged Pat to jiggle his canister while he measured, by experience alone, quantity pooling in the empty bottle. It didn't seem to make sense but it was working.

'Argh! No cigarette here! Please!' commanded Al. The looks on the boys' faces were a comic melange of bafflement and amazement in equal measures. A small tortoise crossed the pine needle carpet hurrying importantly the way of tortoises everywhere.

Tomorrow they would climb Mount Olympus but for today there was one and only one distraction – the deep, translucent Aegean.

The welcome wasn't exactly the one you would hope for.

I had been awake since three, survived the pot holes and peregrination of scorching Serbia, Macedonia and Thessaly. It had become too hot to even sing and I fell silent listening to Austin's big band assembly of complaints. Eventually we turned off at the battered sign for Platamon and tentatively I picked my way down the incline through the parting crowds. That itself should have been a warning.

'We have nothing for you' said the twelve-year-old girl with undisguised derision. The roads had been practically empty and I hadn't been able to figure out why, but the journey from the Macedonian border to Platamon had been protracted and scorching but without incident. The big vibrant welcome that greeted Mum and Dad was absent and other than the profusion of dusty olive trees and an azure and white flag there was little to say I was in Greece at all. I could have been passing along any motorway in the Med.

With rising concern I explained to the side of the girl's head that my parents had loved Castle Camping, not only spending weeks on the way in 1967 but in subsequent years as well. Her father, a neat individual, appeared from the darkness of the reception, took my postcard, listened while I tried to explain again. He circled Austin once without comment or cares for my endeavour and returned to the booth as if I hadn't been there.

The girl looked at me again, 'We still have nothing for you', and her sneer invited me in no uncertain terms to now fuck off. It seems that romance has become tarnished after all.

Stretching along this strip of the Thessaly coast were another ten or more camping sites. Too exhausted to even contemplate searching elsewhere I parked Austin beneath a magnificent olive to tick and groan as he cooled and I set off to find refuge.

It was certainly a lively place. There were hordes of excited people and vehicles clogging the street. I wondered if everyone in Greece was here. Was this why the roads were empty, because they were all here in the splendid sun? Ten gloriously hirsute men were playing a merry game of cards in the shade on the next campsite. They cheerfully informed me that everyone was indeed here as it was the Greek national holiday and that their campsite too was full, but I should keep trying, I would eventually find somewhere as there were campsites from here all the way to Turkey.

Eventually I pulled into a site. The young man at the reception agreed that they could indeed squeeze in a little tent and such a beautiful car. And so I was here in

Platamon; my parents' Elysium vision made physical. When the spiteful North Sea winds pulled at their coats in Ramsgate or Brighton this is what they dreamt of. Freezing August promenades, pensioners and Punch and Judy were but a distant nightmare here.

After making myself comfortable, I strolled to the beach and compared it with the original photos. I ordered a beer that the irritable restaurant matron seemed to begrudge giving me. In a twist she spoke English over-loudly and slowly to me as if she had learnt it from Alf Garnett. The beach, bleached of colour at this time of day, was peopled by thousands of visitors. The tick tock of hundreds of paddle bats kept time with the sun, dividing up the remains of the day into millions of seconds. It was like being in an antiques shop except people were enjoying themselves. There were more umbrellas and games of paddleball than in the 1967 prints but it was most definitely the image trapped in Kodak Gold. Windsurfers had replaced water skiers. Mum and Dad had paid for an afternoon's water skiing with a handful of Great British PG Tips and a couple of cans of Spam. In a land of moussaka and souvlaki how could reprocessed meat have any value? But it did.

As the sun worshippers followed the sun's arc over the restaurant they shuffled around and, sat peacefully with my beer, I was suddenly and horrifying in the sightline of a phalanx of gussets. It wasn't anywhere as good as it might sound. Even the most desperate deviants would, like me, find themselves a little queasy. I returned to the shade of the tent.

I had struggled through Croatia, Serbia and Macedonia with little money, but upon arriving in Greece, a fully-fledged member of the Eurozone, I found myself unable to pay by card. Even in the dark Sar Mountains of Macedonia I had been able to use it if

I needed to but not here. Camping, it seemed, in Greece was a cash-based economy and I would have to walk into town and draw some cash tomorrow. Considering the state of the Greek debt this was probably a very wise move.

At present the Greek debt is roughly 160% of the country's GDP. Politicians have claimed that perks like early retirement age and social care were set in place to lessen the burden that had nearly crushed the spirit of the Greeks. They had fought for independence from the moribund Ottoman Empire, the First and the Second World Wars, Monarchies, the Greek civil war and the brutal Colonels' regime. In 1974 Greece finally got a democracy and abolished its monarchy and joined the EU in 1981. Since then they seem to have been spending nonstop. By the time the government came to power in 2009 and discovered that the previous accountant had been somewhat fudged it was too late. Investors downgraded the Junk bond status and by 2010 the Eurozone and the International Monetary Fund began negotiating a €110 million bail. The first of many, it would seem.

'Today everyone is too clever, too educated. I have been here 35 years and I have seen many changes, everything is not so simple today. Before we built beautiful things, sensitive things. Today, people don't know what they want, they just want. We should live more simply.' Maybe Papa was right.

The skies bled and then darkened to a rich imperial purple. The summer air was thick with pine resin and the residual heat of the day. Between screaming motorbikes racing up and down the entrance, drowsy cicadas attempted a hoarse ballad.

'It is the I Kimisis tis Theotokou, the Assumption of the Holy Virgin where the mother of Christ went to heaven, but as you can see it's not exactly a religious holiday any more.'

Papa took a sip of coffee and looked at Austin. I said the simplicity of Greek life was a draw that my parents were powerless against. That is why they loved it here.

In the deepening darkness Papa was a pale ghost, smartly dressed in slacks and ironed shirt. As the first bats arrived to harvest the insects dancing in the streetlights he chose his words carefully.

'Today they just put plastic in the machine and take what they haven't earned. Then they go fight the police for the right to again take what they haven't earned. So what is the answer? We sell our islands, the beaches to the Germans? Do we sell more? Do we sell the Parthenon, Delphi?'

He sipped his coffee again with all the dignity it is possible to muster with another half-wit on a cheap motorcycle revving and bawling past. He waited until it passed and the silence briefly returned.

'No, simple is better.'

The next morning, keen to pay my bill, get some fresh groceries and escape the tourist crowds I took a walk up over the hill into town. Mum and Dad had done something similar. 'At 3.15 we took a ride into the village to try and get some fresh meat. We were amazed to see a lot of Military around; in fact you could have cut the atmosphere with a knife. We were all three glad to leave.' The Greece of '67 was newly in the grip of the Colonels' Junta, which seized the country about the time the trio, sat in their Welsh pub, were complaining about the weather.

Greece had fought hard for its independence from German occupation and their stance after liberation was a very emphatic anti-communist one. From VE to the Sixties the anti-communist resolve crystallised. The Lyndon B. Johnson administration in the US whole-heartedly supported this position even to the point that when it seemed likely that the very popular centralist Georges might win the 1967 elections he was seen as a Red. With a nod from the CIA and led by George Papadopoulos the colonels seized power on the morning of 21st April 1967.

Five months later Mum and Dad trundled across the border very pleasured to be out of the oppressive Tito regime but seemingly unaware of just how dangerous their position was. The Greeks themselves shielded them from this. Greece was under military law. Tanks were on the streets in Athens, but this was the age of the Cold War, there had been tanks on the streets in Yugoslavia; it had become a little commonplace. LBJ and the CIA were happy with this ultra right pro-NATO as a bulwark wedged tight up against the Iron Curtain. Colonels would cling to power, the Turkish invasion of Cyprus would finally bring it down seven years later.

With Tito's dislike for Stalin and the Junta keen to paint liberals as Reds, the West had successfully robbed Russia of access to the Mediterranean. Although they seemed to have arrived now. The tiny number of 2000 inhabitants of Platamon swelled to a staggering 120,000 during the peak season. Those who aren't Greek are from the Warsaw Pact and Russia today. Few Brits and westerners come here these days, preferring the Peloponnese and the idyllic isle beyond.

The original crew had stopped to look at the 12th century Byzantine castle with its flying beetles and collected a pet tortoise on the way up. At the time Mum planned to keep it but her conscience got the better of her and she returned the 'adorable little thing' to the roadside where she had found it.

As I arrived a coach crushed the gravel of the car park and vomited an impossible number of sightseers. I figured that the castle had been there since the Byzantines had built it to subjugate the ancient trade routes between Thessaly to Macedonia and so I could visit it later, but somehow never did.

Turning my back on the gods on Mount Olympus and heading along the old train line into the town I found a lazy Sunday morning as an antidote to the hordes.

The town was peopled by stately gentlemen and ladies in their Sunday best. After returning from morning mass they drank coffee with measured sips and nibbled pastries with equal care. I wandered down to the front to have breakfast and watch the swimming heads trim across the sea. Those not at prayer or gossiping in the cafés were scattered about the beach. I settled at a table and waited for someone to take my order. Two snorkelers, heads down, fins striking as much air as Aegean, were on a collision course and while I waited for this modest entertainment to play out I ordered coffee and pastries. Wavelets kissed the pebbles, with the scat, scat, scat of lazy brushes on a snare.

Greece seems to run through my family like the

veins in marble. For others it might be Spain or the US of A, but for us it was Greece. It is difficult sometimes to separate those tales of my parents' from my own faded recollections. My first memories are of an inflatable blue dolphin that went everywhere with me on Corfu. I learned to swim with him, shared my watermelon and pomegranate with him; I even took it to see the village goats being milked amongst the tinkling of a hundred hircine bells in the neighbouring village when we were invited. Mr Dolphin's maniacal smile sent the pungent billie goat into angry pirouettes.

After this my greatest possessions were the tiny ding fins and mask my Dad bought from Crete. In the other fifty weeks we were restricted to our home in North Wales I would, with the aid of my diving kit, scuba dive around the houses, fins flapping against lino and horrid brown floral carpets that seemed like a good idea in the Seventies. Dad would finally get home and wrestle the mask, fins and washing-up bottle aqualungs off a sleepy child, carrying him upstairs to sleep off his decompression with a head full of octopuses and sharks.

Bath times were surrounded by sea urchin shells and a massive conch, bought at the wharf and carried carefully back to grey Britain to add just the faintest physicality to the daydreams.

My Greekling father, always quick to tan and with an unruly mop that never bleached or lightened, was renamed Paddy the Greek by his family. We grew up with a soundtrack of jazz and Mikis Theodorakis. In the dark years after the Junta passed Army decree Number 13 and arrested, imprisoned and finally exiled Theodorakis, his Zorba's theme was the soundtrack to a slightly barmy scuba diving child. Mum began to worry about me.

Over the years Gerald Durrell's My Family and

Other Animals became the family book of choice. Achilles, Heracles and Zeus marched and fought through my bedtime stories. Zorba on LP was replaced with tape, then CD as Dad wore each one out. It played in the house, in the car and even from his rickety shed.

As the two snorkelers threatened to crack heads but disappointedly pulled up at the last second, I had begun to feel very emotional and was thankful for the sunglasses when the waiter delivered my breakfast. It was like a tap being turned on, I was amazed at just how early and deeply this feisty little country had settled into my soul.

Brake-seatbelt-bum shuffle – cash. Now in reverse. Travel ten miles and repeat

Brake-seatbelt-bum shuffle – cash.
Brake-seatbelt-bum shuffle – cash.
Brake-seatbelt-bum shuffle – cash.

All the way from Platamon through the Gates of Thermopylae to the chaos of Athens this was the rhythm Austin and I followed through the seemingly thousands of Greece toll booths. I handed over fistfuls of euros like some benevolent patriarch casting coins from the window as we passed through a world bleached of colour. Only the Aegean, a deep Yves Klein international blue, seemed impervious to the hammering sun.

The road tolls were getting expensive although it was an acceptable alternative to the wacky races of Macedonia's potholes. I felt by the time I reached Athens that I was personally shoring up the quivering Greek economy. German chancellor Angela Merkel and French president Sarkozy fear that if Greece is allowed to drop out or go bankrupt then the dominoes of Portugal, Italy and Ireland will be next. This cavalcade scares everyone, the Americans, the Chinese, but above all Europeans. No one can afford for it to fail. In 2007 the Germans increased their retirement age from 65 to 67 while the Greeks, who retire at 58, have been agitating to get it lowered further. But something has to give. The bailouts have done little to staunch the fiscal bleeding. The austerity measures voted on by subsequent leaderships have failed or in many cases failed to be implemented. What started out as a half joke has finally solidified into a real possibility. In the near future Greece might well have a garage sale to end all garage sales. It is speculated that bargains on the table may be previously untouched islands and peninsulas, the whole of the exiled king's property portfolio, including his string of antique cars rusting outside his mansion, and even access to the Pantheon and other holies by media companies.

Why a media company would wish to film in what is ostensibly a building site is beyond me but the next morning as I stood with the other tourists I was still awestruck by the authority of the place. I ambled about the Acropolis with its tour groups, construction workers and stiff shoving wind. There is no longer the opportunity to walk in and around the pillars and stones as my parents had done. There was little that tourists could do wrong in the new regime's eyes. Tourist police even saluted as they drove past. Today, like Stonehenge, the Parthenon is fenced off, and having seen the damage wrought by tourism across the archaeological sites of the world I'm whole-heartedly in favour of it.

When the permeating aura of blinding white finally got too much and the heat had shrink wrapped my t-shirt to my torso I wandered through the baked stones of Athens searching for shade amongst the olives and tourist shops, looking for book shops to buy a guide to

Turkey. Athens is a great place for being side tracked. Every corner or street offers you a tantalising glimpse of something marvellous – the Agora and the Temple of Hephaitos, or maybe the Theatre of Dionysus or the prison of Socrates, so it took a good while until I washed up at a small restaurant on a side road near Syntagma Square, the only one it seemed not the slightest bit interested in my custom. With uncharacteristic surliness the waitress took my order while I wrote postcards. The search for postcards had been a strange one. They seemed to be left-over stock from the original trip, faded and horribly old-fashioned, I made hilarious comment on this on cards for Jimmy and my parents.

As I ate my lunch tourists went about the purchasing of rosary beads, mythical figurines and sallow icons but had I been sat there six weeks earlier lunch would have been interrupted by tear gas and stun grenades. Through the clouds the Athens riot police would charge and hammer me from my chair with truncheons and batons.

On 28th June as the politicians inside the parliament building sought to ratify the next round of austerity measures demanded by the EU and the IMF in return for a second bailout of €130 billion, police and protestors clashed violently on the steps outside. As the riot cops sought to clean the Syntagma Square, running battles and skirmishes spread out into nearby streets and as the fog of tear gas and white rage descended it seemed everyone was at risk. The brutality of the police was broadcast live across the world's media as their politicians voted to accept the next round of restriction. When the clouds cleared there had been €500,000 worth of damage according to the Greek Skai channel and nearly 750 causalities visited the hospital over the next two days. The austerity measures bill was passed anyway, protest continued in many cities including Thessaloniki where they had peacefully dispersed only a week before I arrived. Prime Minister George Papandreou eventually lost his seat to pressure from protesters and the opposition, but saving Greece from economic chaos will be a poison chalice to the foreseeable future.

We had checked out early and Katarina, the new manager, had refused to let me pay for my pitch. 'it is a lovely thing you do. For your parents and for you.' Mum and Dad had loved Camping Nea Kiffissia and the munificence of George. They adored his sense of hospitably and to them he embodied in his tall lanky frame everything that was good about Greece and the Greeks. 'My father was a lovely man. Kind and generous,' said Katrina as I showed her some photographs from 1967. 'We have new windows and more plants today but it is the same.' I tried to pay once more and again she refused insisting that it was a special day, and so the spirit of Greece that was so loved by Dad still lives on a while longer.

'Where are you from?' yelled the old man from the next car. The dawn was just maturing as I arrived at the first junction.

A little startled I replied, 'From Britain.'

'I know that! I had a Wolsey 63!' He had eyebrows like a stag beetle.

'Much posher,' I yelled back over the traffic and offered an enthusiastic thumbs up at his big beaming face. He nodded his approval, ignored the red light and set off down the highway in the opposite direction.

Austin and I turned north and left Athens to its growing morning rush hour. Very quickly the traffic fell away, thinning further with each metre. The sun rose until we began to pass through those blissful voids when we were the only vehicle for miles in any direction.

That other great lover of the Greeks, Patrick Leigh Fermor, claimed that 'All horsepower corrupts' yet he had never had the joy of driving happy little Austin along the Aegean coast. This is what I had fantasised about when planning the trip. Long slow arcs and curves in and out of the coast hemmed between the sea and slopes. The skies crystal clear and the hot air, laded with dust and the sea salt, whipping excitedly through the interior mixing with the mélange of leather and oil. It would chase Charlie Parker or Ella Fitzgerald around the cab playfully before escaping out the open window back into the olive groves beyond.

Austin twittered like a little bird, his usual percussion syncopated into a sweet chirping as if we had a songbird on the back seat. It didn't matter that we had no speedo, oil or temperature gauges nor that the windscreen wiper motors had died. We didn't care that the steering was heavy yet vague and whimsical; nor that the brakes could be described in the same manner. It was as perfect as it was possible to be and, as I'd promised myself in the early daydreams, I put on my sunglasses, I hung my arm out of the window and tapped the bodywork in time to Chet or Charlie or Nat and I knew there and then that no one had been this cool, in this place, since 1967.

We cruised through the lands of my childhood reading. Through the languid morning we swept past the sacred mountains of the fiery centaur, the birthplace of heroic Jason and the home of the Argo and on to the bloody Gates of Thermopylae where the Persian tide was stemmed and democracy saved. On through the white heat of the day we made our way north until we paused in the shade of the Vale of Tempe where Apollo cavorted with his muses in a manner deemed too base even for the corrupt pleasures of Mount Olympus. In 1967 this is as far as the original Austin got before it coughed, sputtered and in a cloud of indignant steam pulled off the road.

You might want to argue that Austin and I had cheated as he should have gone to the mechanics in Germany but as far as we were concerned, with the exception of the death slide in Austria, we were both still ticking along nicely. Under the rustling plane trees we parked up and celebrated with a warm bottle of water. The only sound was the gurgle of the River Pineios sauntering quietly through the lush gorge bound for the thirsty Aegean.

It is a beautiful spot and popular with the tourists scouring the country in their hunger for culture. It has played host to lusty deities and scanty nymphs, to brutal warriors and was beloved most of all by gentle poets. The modernist American Madison J Cawein whose Waste Land is considered the inspiration for TS Elliot's more famous piece of the same name wrote blissfully about the Vale of Tempe and of

The loamy odor of the turfy heat,
Breathed warm from every field and wood retreat,
Is as if spirits passed on flowery feet
That indescribable
Aroma of the woods one knows so well

While the gorge has reverberated with the sandals and jack boots of Persian, Byzantine, Turk and German armies it is almost as silent today as it was in 1967 when Jimmy was packed off to hitchhike to a mechanic's or Platamon or whichever came first. Fixing the fan belt hadn't remedied anything so he disappeared around the corner beneath the naked limestone peaks thumb held high in his cheerful Bradford manner.

Almost the moment Jim left a van pulled into the laurels' shade next to the car with a stencil proclaiming to be the Greek AA. A large bearded mechanic bounded out. Short and stocky Yannis' greying whiskers seemed to continue across his shoulder and back and along the length of his arms. He joshed and joked with Mum and Dad from beneath the bonnet. With a cry of victory he surfaced with the offending part, the thermostat! With a 'Broke, Kaput' he tossed the amputated part over his shoulder into the River Pineios where it possibly still lies today. He refused to take their drachma, instead happily accepting 20 Gold Leaf cigarettes. They were what Mum's father smoked. She didn't like them, preferring her Senior Service, so the crew had used them as additional currency. Yannis followed them up the road where they collected a very surprised Jimmy and headed off to Platamon.

Austin and I planned to spend one more night there too as we headed to Kavala and the Turkish border. It would be unfair to judge a place on a summer bank holiday. Having grown up in a tourist region, I know people and places are rarely seen at their best when dealing with a rampancy of weekenders. But the place was still shell shocked after the hammering it had taken, only the dust dancing in tiny zephyrs moved. Yet as much as my parents had loved it, present day Platamon was not for me so the next morning we took the E75 highway north heading along the coast to Kavala where the last king of Greece, Constantine II, prepared his doomed counter coup against the Colonels and my parents had paused before crossing into Asia Minor.

Austin is not a car built for this century; not its traffic, its red, amber and greens, its short tempers or its

148

challenging parking. After a morning of almost blissful motoring with Steve McQueen delusions, the knotted streets of Kavala were a nightmarish ordeal. We pinballed around the one-way system looking for the Tourist Information. We circled three times before some miracle delivered us to a spot outside an ATM and twenty metres from the office. The girl paused in her coffee to give me the two options, both, of course in opposite directions, but the Batis fitted the description of the original camp so we went there.

It was a beautiful spot. Everything a family could hope for. The brochure stated that it was 'a tempting motivation for visiting northern Greece' and promised that I would be 'impressed by the sufficiency and functionality' of the place. The camping bays are neatly retained before pivot hedges and the sea was as turquoise as you could hope for. The beach had a testudo of umbrellas, a pool, free wifi, and a choice of bars. Other than the party until four in the morning I couldn't find anything to grumble about. Like the site at Zell Am See it hadn't changed a great deal. It too had improved security and facilities, both had met the pyroclastic flow of tourism that the Colonels unleashed on the country and had survived and thrived. But it lacked the home charm of Camping Nea Kiffissia. It had everything I wanted yet I couldn't quite relax there. It was too close to a Club Med, too clinical and perfect. I drank my overpriced beer in the olive's shade and after a cooling swim spent the afternoon, sleepy in the heat, watching the ants climb my guy ropes and between passages from Nikos Kazantzakis' Zorba the Greek contemplated Istanbul.

Zorba: You've got everything except one thing: madness! A man needs a little madness, or else...

Chapter Eleven – Red Sails in the Sunset (Nat King Cole)

Monday 14th August – Kartelepe/Turkey

Pat and I went over the road to the little shop to get some Eggs and Tomatoes for breakfast. (One tomato weighted over 1¼ lbs). We all got ready to go into Istanbul. We picked up a Mini bus at the bus stop and had a nightmare drive to the Old City Wall. We found the Bazaars after a tramp up and down the streets. They were fabulous, I've never seen a place quite like it. Arcades by the millions. Jewellery shops cramped full of gold, leather shops packed tight with coats, suits and jackets. I could easily have spent every penny I had.

Mileage for the day 143   Acc. Mileage 2975

An outrageous black Buick screamed a round of Colonel Bogey and nearly knocked Pam off her feet. The taxis crawled unctuously about the city streets like monstrous black beetles.

The driver leaned hopefully out the window calling them, but Pam just waved him away as politely as she could. 'Let's go and get some lunch' but she hadn't needed to say anything as Pat was already guiding them across the cobbles towards the Galata Bridge and the shimmering Golden Horn.

Jimmy fiddled with his camera, firing the shutter and winding it over and over again, not quite ready to risk another roll of film after yesterday's trouble in the Blue Mosque. Still there was always this afternoon he thought as Pat led them past the Aya Sophie with its srummage of blushing cupolas.

The calls of gulls and ferries guided them through the last alleyways until the horizon opened up glittering like a pasha's riches. The Golden Horn was no less busy than the souks had been; ferries, yachts, fishing boats and tankers elbow and squabble importantly across the Bosphorus and Marmara Sea.

Between the odours of oily docks, the mixing of three waters and belching car fumes squeezed the delicate promise of grilled fish.

Along the rails anglers snatched silver catches from the dancing waters and with a slash, wash and sizzle the fish found themselves forced between two slices of bread.

'You Americas?'

'English,' said Pam through steaming mouthfuls of mackerel sandwich.

'Him's America,' thumbed the chef towards a small crowd of policemen on the steps down to the water's edge. They appeared to be struggling with a brightly decorated sack. 'Him's Hippies.' The wake of a passing ferry was making life difficult for the police. 'Him's no money. No blood,' he chuckled sinisterly. If they had been superstitious they might have seen it as an omen. Perhaps they should have been superstitious.

The last ten miles to the border saw Austin and I alone with the rusting dawn and a wondering mind. In the next hour we would be entering the Levant, that most mystical oriental jumble of Turkey, Syria, Jordan, Lebanon, Cyprus, Israel and Egypt. All, in their own major or minor way, would have a role to play over the next few weeks. Yet it was hard to believe that events hundreds of miles away, across not only the Hellespont, but the steely Mediterranean, could ripple out across the waves to affect the passage of a Persian blue Cambridge and its sleepy driver.

We rattled through the silence of the golden morning, before the sun bleaches the fields and blends the skies of Thrace into the sea. Trailing rust and fine blue smoke, Austin and I drove through groups of storks stood in the bare fields like unemployed immigrants. On eastwards past shepherds and solar farms and kestrels hard at work.

At the border Mustafa cheerfully checked my passport and sent me to get a visa. The stern visa official with a profile like a goshawk took my Turkish lira, stamped my visa and offered me a mint. The grey haired Burham was the Green Card man. He suggested that I stop in Şarköy rather than Ipsala, emphatic that I should bypass central Istanbul. 'Do not drive there, you will be eaten I am a hundred per cent sure' and then sent me on with my paperwork to the woman in the office. Sat beneath an oversized photograph of a timid waterfall I won her undying enmity when 'Austin Cambridge' failed to appear on her database. Snatching up my paperwork she stormed off to her boss who apparently told her to input it by hand. She returned glaring at me with undisguised venom and jabbed spitefully at her keyboard. Still she avenged herself with a £55 fee. Outside, Burham amiably checked my paperwork again, fed me sweets and gave me directions to a Kamp Yeri in Şarköy. Giving me his phone number he insisted I call him when he returned to Istanbul in a few days. 'You must see the Bosphorus with a local, it is the only way.' Then with a final thump of his stamp I was free to roam Turkey as I pleased.

The most evocative line of the whole journal was written about Ipsala; Friday 11th August: 'During the evening I saw my first Camel train.'

There was little left of Ipsala. The decades had leached the colour and life from the town. No one stopped here any more; not camels, campers nor the world at large it seemed. After forty-five minutes of searching for a Kamp Yeri, Austin and I left the weather beaten faces and, turning back onto the highway, took the advice we had been given at the border.

An hour later we turned off the E-5 at Tekirdağ, and took the meandering side road through fields of penitent sunflowers and wilting tobacco towards the coast, until it delivered us into the chaotic heart of Şarköy. It seemed like it took the rest of the day to escape. Around and around Austin and I struggled, lost amongst the old ottoman mansions and new tourist flats, stopping for tractors and fruit carts and dusty family saloons.

Turkey's tourist board proudly boasts that Şarköy has 60km of beach, making it the twelfth longest in the world, and that it holds an EU Blue Flag for water quality. But as I passed it for the fifth time it remained as uninspiring as the previous four viewings. Eventually I gave up on the Kamp Yeri and collapsed into a modest motel on the seafront to kill the afternoon and took a windy walk along the promenade looking for an ATM. Seafront flags snapped and danced above ugly tourist horse carts bedecked in chintz and drawn by skinny nags. The beach utterly failed to compete with those of Greece only a day's drive away. It is favoured by the upper working class and lower middle classes of Istanbul but ultimately seems to lack any class.

As evening drew on Şarköy began to grow on me a little more. In the back streets away from the more awful tourist tripe the fruit sellers sold delicate looking cobnuts and acorns amongst the bombastic melons and blushing peaches. Old men visited their clubs for tea or the barber's to gossip while bootblacks squatted with lavishly ornate boxes as the last notes of the Adhan warbled through the evening air. I found a seat at a quiet restaurant and after three attempts managed to order the local specialty of balık çorbası, fish soup, for dinner and while aromas of warm bread and bubbling stews filled the evening air I watched the sun squeeze through the clouds on its way west.

I failed to sleep any better in a bed than on a roll mat and awoke feeling lost and lonely, but at breakfast I fell into conversation with Ahmet, a professor of economics, soon to be retired. Neat with a kind face he joined me at the table which is where his graceful wife, Ahyalniz, found him deep in conservation with a straggly stranger. She taught in a primary school and the pair had some land above Şarköy where they were growing walnuts. Ahmet had learned his superlative English when he travelled the UK for the first time in 1967–8; he then went on to complete his Masters in Bradford about the time Jimmy got home after the trip. They were adamant that I should avoid sprawling Istanbul at all costs even going as far as to give me a new map. Pushing away the debris of breakfast they traced a route to Kartalepe that would take me around the worst of the city's snarling traffic.

On the way out of town I stopped to refuel as I did every travel day and Turkish hospitality stalled me once again. The station owner's son had studied at university in Ireland. He insisted I stop for breakfast or at least a 'cuppa' and warned me again about driving in the city. 'You must go around' he said while offering the sugar bowl.

Everyone was in agreement about my day's route, me most of all, but when I recognised the Theodosius II Walls I knew I'd made a horrible mistake somewhere. Sat at the lights with the walls on one side and the steely blue of Sea of Marmara, punctuated with its tugs and ferries, I felt like I was perched on top of Niagara Falls in a pedalo; you might survive but you wouldn't want to stake your life on it.

Then the lights snapped red, amber, green. I was off. Dragged along in the torrent and your only hope is to keep flailing your arms and gasping for air. The surge pulled me along the coast and I knew from a previous visit that sooner or later I would reach the Yeşilköy Feneri Lighthouse at which point I was about as fucked as it was possible to be.

Years before, at the end of several months hitching along the Silk Road, I had arrived in Istanbul and instantly fallen for the city. You may want to argue that after months in dusty and oppressive Uzbekistan, Turkmenistan and in particular Iran anywhere would have seemed paradise. I had somehow been persuaded by a befuddled Iranian dentist to be his porter but the instant my penance was complete I collapsed into the nearest café and finally removed months of congealed goat and sheep fat from the roof of my mouth. I had wandered blissfully through the alleyways and palaces, the museums, mosques and mayhem of modern Istanbul in a daze of confusion, fatigue and exhilaration at reaching my goal. A rose tinted memory for sure, but the terror of the braying Turkish drivers haunted me. Valiantly clinging to a Bakelite steering wheel I snatched painfully up and down through the gears. The Austin's heavy chassis fetched and rolled on its ancient springs seemingly without rhythm as we struggled along Kennedy Caddesi (named after JFK). The horns and revs, crunching gears and squealing brakes rose and fell with the almost imperceptible pulse of a Thelonious Monk improvisation.

Austin was slow off the line and equally sluggish to brake. Attempting the rapid double dip clutch-neutral-clutch and into first in an attempt to get the cogs to synchronise while trying to read road signs wasn't going well. Then it was clutch-neutral-accelerate into second on the way up again. All the while the dissonant Turkish sun hammered down on a fifty year old thermostat as a horse cart pushed in front forcing me to jam my foot hard on the brakes. When my chain of profanities died away I had an instant to realise we were in the serrate shadow of the grand Ottoman Topkapi Palace high above. As soon as we entered Sultanahmet we were in the hands of fate.

A split second's indecision found us funnelled deeper into the mosque and minaret saturated Sultanahmet. We seemed to be on Ishakpasa Caddesi when at a roundabout we turned right and suddenly found ourselves trawling slowly through the congestion between the twin splendours of the Aya Sophie and the Blue Mosque, where Jim's camera jammed. The traffic was slowing to a walking pace as it drew me slowly past.

In 1967 the crew had been able to park anywhere at the side of the road. In fact to make sure they remembered where they parked they left their Austin right outside the Blue Mosque. There had been only a handful of other cars and these had been almost exclusively large American Buicks making a living as taxis. The occasional Volkswagen or Citroen punctuated this scene but Dad thought it strange how American the place felt.

Like Greece the Americans had been pumping millions into Turkey as their bulwark against the Soviets and the dreaded Reds. In fact the American placement of Jupiter nuclear missiles in Turkey in 1958 had been a key catalyst in the 1962 Cuban Missile Crisis where the belligerent première Nikita Khrushchev and equally bombastic JFK brought the world to the edge of annihilation. After a heated stand-off Kennedy relented and secretly removed the Turkish missiles, much to the chagrin of the host nation, while the Russian ships turned back to port. Khrushchev's public backing down would ultimately cost him his place as the first amongst equals in Moscow while wily JFK met his end a year later in Dallas.

As the traffic sped up I thought I was looking at my last days, but there above, in the afternoon shimmer was the Galata Bridge. It should not have been passing above me. Again I had made a wrong turn. We were now driving north up the Golden Horn coast. Stop, start, stop, start, we pushed on hoping for a turning space before reaching Bulgaria.

After three more attempts, boiled and disoriented, we connected with the rush hour commuters heading home. We crossed the Bosphorus leaving behind Thrace and Europe, we were finally speeding along in the right direction if not the right road. I regretted complaining about the red lights and the arrhythmic pulses of the traffic earlier. Here was a near nonstop torrent of howling traffic hell bent on getting home. If the morning had been the abrupt pauses and hesitations of Monk then the afternoon was the frenzied nonstop cadenza of Art Tatum, and from the skill of the driving the same gift of blindness.

The Turkish Nobel Laureat Orhan Pamuk said in his Istanbul: Memories and the City that 'the first thing I learned at school was that some people are idiots; the second thing I learned was that some are even worse.' It seems those people grew up and bought cars and were this evening rushing to get home.

Eyes strained for overtakers to the right and bastardly buses to the left I listened for genuine threats and warnings hidden amongst the purely bolshie and cantankerous rush hour cacophony. Then the rush hour began and it became a mental inundation.

How we got to Kartal, where the original party rested blissfully after their dalliance of spice bazaars and gold souks, was a blur of unrepentant anarchy.

Fearing terrible consequence from the rush hour rally I yanked the steering wheel and bounced terrifyingly off the road into a parking space outside the first and only hotel. I think I sat in the car for possibly ten hours waiting for my road rage to dissipate. Placing a brick behind the wheel I staggered into the reception and collapsed into the first room they offered me.

❧

'No, no campsites here. Only us,' said Soner at breakfast. A little research revealed that Kartal and its campsites have been swallowed up by the lahar of the republic's development and Istanbul's growth. Immediately after the Second World War the district developed into an industrial region. There were still campsites along the Marmara Sea then but with the construction of the commuter trains to the Haydarpaşa Station on the Sea of Marmara in 1974 the whole area was bought up by developers and the factories have been pushed back. 'There is a ferry tomorrow morning. It is Ramadan at the moment. Mr Button I suggest you take it. Timetables sometimes change.' And with Soner's advice I got tentatively back into Austin and fired up the engine and pushed off for the ferry to Yalova and the search for the last of the campsites of the trip.

I paced fitfully up and down the ferry until we docked in Yalova. The guidebook said that the town had been hammered with an earthquake in 1991, although I wouldn't have known as I passed through bound for Bursa. It was a beautiful ride up through the hills, rich and verdant in the creases of the valleys, but it was the beginning of the end of my parents' trip. About 100 miles east of Bursa the furious tectonic aggression of the Eurasian, African, Arabian and the Anatolian plate ground angrily together and the resulting calamity was the Mudurnu earthquake. Just a month before, on 22nd July, the North Anatolian Fault reduced 5200 homes and buildings to little more than bare bricks, but thankfully only eighty-six lives were lost in the tragedy. The road infrastructure was torn apart and as they passed through the hills the roads 'made the wheels square' Dad said and Mum recorded in her diary 'How the car didn't fall to bits I shall never know.'

I, too, was concerned about the state of my Austin. The damage I had done during the wacky races through and around Istanbul and its seven hills had added a wobble to the steering and a new percussive paradiddle over the rear arc. And with this added stress I came to the conclusion that I hated Bursa.

The small town had metastasised during the same period that had seen Kartal swallowed. Now it was the fourth biggest city in the country. It certainly had the traffic to prove it. I aimed for the tumble of domes that crowned the Grand Mosque Ulu Camii. It was a long confusing drive in from the pale countryside and once caught in the whirlpool of the one-way system it was impossible to get free. Dense shoals of battered vehicles circled past the covered market and Ulu Camii. And with nerves still not recovered from Istanbul it was frustrating and terrifying. It was midday, the heat pounded down vertically and radiated up from the concrete and the stop, start, panic. When he overheated Austin did not throw a hissing fit of steam but rather a curmudgeonly stall. I restarted him and we crept forward a few metres before he died again. The mosque was within a stone's throw and we couldn't get there. Filling the air with expletives, I pulled over again and threw open the bonnet. Reaching for the radiator cap I pressed hard down without thinking and smelt rather than felt the searing and melting of my palm to the metal. 'What have you done to your hand?' It seemed to have been the first civil question I had been asked all day. We had struggled through the traffic and after finding a parking space in the rabbit warren of old Bursa I had met the rudest tourist information service anywhere in the world. I had returned to Austin with a temper to match the temperature. He sat precarious and forlornly outside a teashop on a slope with a brick behind each wheel. An angry welt of carmine and white had begun to blister and I imagined I could make out 'Desserrer lentement. Remove slowly' branded across the skin. It throbbed.

'Please. Sit. Tea here.' Macedonian Meto offered me one of his awful Turkish cigarettes. 'Me, I Makedonija. Them mans local. Them buggery,' he said and they all nodded cheerfully and saluted me with their glasses. We settled at the wooden table, its plastic coating tattered and scratched, it once sung the glories of the Aya Sophia. It was around midday; the tattered awning offered a little respite. Uncertain how to reply I raised my glass, the tea was as light and honey coloured as the light pouring down the walls. I toasted 'Macedonia good' and then with a great deal less conviction 'Buggery. Good.'

'Yah. Him. Sophie,' I smiled and nodded back 'Merhaba Sophie, As-Salamu Alaykum.' I was almost certain that Sophie was male, he/she resembled a ninety year old coal miner fresh from a shift.

The next man, young, bespectacled, recently escaped from a library, was 'Varna', his neighbour was also Sophie, and his too. The penultimate drinker was 'Blagoevgrad' and finally, another Sophie. Sophie certainly seemed a poplar name in Bursa and with another salute to Buggery and Macedonia they put pistachio baklava on the table. I looked through into the kitchen to thank the cook and noticed the poster on the wall. Bulgaria was emblazoned across a snow-clad scene of the Boyana Church in the capital Sofia. During the communist revolutions of the Sixties as the Iron Curtain swept in, hundreds of thousands of Bulgarian Turks fled the old Ottoman enclaves for the safety of Anatolia. There was little room for free thought in the new regime and Islam was one aspect Premier Zhivkov felt strongly about. Nearly fifty thousand settled in Bursa.

With that mystery solved I raised my glass a final time and offered 'Cheers to Makedonija and cheers to Buggery!'

Chapter Twelve – Good Morning Heartache (Billie Holiday)

Thursday 17th August – Kartalepe/Turkey

The road was good until we turned off for Bursa. My
God I've never seen a road like it, in parts it was
practically nonexistent and where there was a surface
you couldn't see through the dust, 45 miles of this, poor
old Pat was fed up to the teeth with it. How the car
didn't fall to bits I shall never know.'
Mileage for the day 160   Acc. Mileage 3135

*The biker looked proudly at his paint can rather than
embarrassed.*

*'You just put the new stuff on top, mix it in and cook
it again?' Pam asked incredulously. 'That looks awful,
good luck to you.'*

*'Yep' her stomach couldn't really take much more.
She hadn't let on to Pat and Jim how wretched she felt.
The smell of the Afghan coats as they hung like drying
corpses over the chain link fence was awful. The idiots*

hadn't even checked that they were properly cured and now a week later the smell of rotting goat hung in the still heat clogging nostrils and turning stomachs.

Kevin was taking his bike east heading for Iran and India before 'these new hippy guys stunk it up with their patchouli oil and these fucking goat coats. It's you Beetle fault apparently'. She left him with Jim to talk about motorbikes. 'The road south is fucking terrible and even if you are suicidal enough to persuade the Syrians to give you some sort of visa, they'll want £1000 indemnity from you. Fuck that! I'm heading to Tehran, it's much more fucking civilised than the south.'

Pam rested in the tent; the air was thick and choking. She'd slept most of the night and early hours of the day. Jim was petrified about the Third Arab-Israeli War. He was certain it would flare up again even if they were calling it the 'Six Day War'. He wanted to go home. Pam hadn't said as much but she wanted the same. Pat fretted over the car. The trip down had been horrendous. He too hadn't said as much but their momentum had faltered. They had no plans to head further east even if the car would take them. If the road south was barred then maybe it was a sign. Pat called to say lunch was ready. She didn't know if she could stand up let alone eat anything. Maybe it was time to head back to Greece.

This is what a kebab should evoke. Rather than drunken evenings in rainy Britain the heat of day should be fading as the western skies darken. The canon has fired to allow the faithful to eat after another day's Ramadan fasting. The echo of the evening calls to pray still flowing out over the city. Rich grilled lamb fattened on the thyme-choked slopes sizzles under its thick tomato sauce. Bats swirl about the twelve cupolas of the Seljuk Ulu Camii.

My mood had improved after a pleasant evening wandering about the 14th century souk, dining on the local Iskender kebabs and a necessary trip to the barber's there was little to keep me any longer in Bursa. The stress of earlier had faded in the knowledge of the day in front of me. The journey particularly over the last few days had begun to feel like a penance, but now my parents had turned west again for a slow leisurely return to the UK, one that would be equally as exciting as the one down, one with smugglers and hospital visits.

The £1000 indemnity asked by Syria for an opportunity to cross a still smouldering warzone was out of the question. Even with the help of my Uncle Michael and the extra smuggled in Dad's socks they had left Belgium with only £600. They had nothing like that by the time they reached Bursa. If I were to be offered the same opportunity it would be a staggering £15,000 in today's money. Anyway everyone expected for it to flare up again.

The Israeli pre-emptive strike at the poorly trained and supplied Egyptian air defences had been disastrous for the Arabs. Israel claiming that President Nasser and his allies Jordan and Syria were massing for an invasion, almost every last Israeli jet screamed out of their bases with the dawn on the 5th June and pulverised the large modern Egyptian air force. The Egyptians had 420 Russian MiG 21s but were taken completely by surprise; the Israelis destroyed eighty per cent of their planes in a matter of hours as they sat on the tarmac. With a return east to base for refuelling the Israelis spent the afternoon neutering the Syrian and Jordanian forces too. It had been a humiliating and degrading defeat for the Arab forces. Egypt lost the whole of the

Sinai peninsular although they would get it back eventually. Israel also gained the fertile farmlands of the Golan Heights from Syria, the West Bank from Jordan, as well as the Gaza Strip from Palestine, and after a week of brutal air and land combat Israel found itself three times the size it had been just a week before. The still smouldering remains of the Arab forces testified that Israel could and would defend its right to exist, by force if necessary.

Leaving Bursa behind, and with a forgettable overnight stop in a self-aggrandising hotel on the edge of Ankara, Austin and I headed south and east across the Anatolia steppe and a chance to contemplate our next step.

There would be no more hours wasted in fretful anguish searching industrial parks, housing estates or wastelands of the ghosts of campsites. Every decision good or bad was now mine as I attempted to succeed where they failed. I now had a blank canvas. Refugees were pouring over the Syrian border, the fighting and protests continued to escalate and no one wanted to use the words 'civil' and 'war'. The advice from the Foreign Office continued to be 'get the hell out by any means'. I couldn't cross the border into Syria, so with only a single choice left to me I turned south with the aim of reaching the coast and crossing to Cyprus.

Heading out on to the central Anatolian plateau bound for the Aksaray Province, we skirted the glistening white slab that is the Tuz Gölü, the salt lake, pushing on through a heat persistent enough to reduce Turkey's second biggest lake to a flat bed of hypersaline powder. The world contracted to dichromatic pastel blue and glimmering white as the road works switched us from one side to the other and back, guiding us with a million cones as occasionally a donkey and rider minced along the edge or a flock of sheep threatened to avalanche across the otobahn. The bare fields fed melons what they could not get from the sun.

We sang and chatted. Almost from the first night I had begun talking to Austin and maybe it was the heat, the boredom, the loneliness or just the cabin fever of long hours driving, but Austin had begun to answer back. He wasn't a great conversationalist. He merely chipped in with an 'Okidoki daddio', 'S'cool, cat' or such like. It was, with the exception of petrol stops, the sum total of my daily conversation.

The heat haze filled in the potholes letting them melt into the tarmac as you approached. The mind has a lot of time to wander through this endless desolation. Thousands of miles of crumpled brown hill. Hamlets and towns hunkered in the hollows, waiting, it seemed, but for what I couldn't guess. Occasionally there was a false horizon of bruised clouds; I never reached them. İ was daydreaming or planning or scheming when there was a flash of lights in the mirror and the unmistakable blue and white of a police car. This was it. This was as far as I got. İ pulled out my paperwork file. So far, by not telling anyone that my papers weren't fully in order I had blagged my way through every previous checkpoint and border. Yet now there would be no getting away from it. I had deliberately stuffed all the papers into a single bursting plastic file. The obvious stuff was on top but I gambled no one would want to be bothered going through the lot. But traffic police have little else to entertain themselves with during the long work day…

We pulled into a layby, lifted the mirror and watched the policeman get out of his car with his note pad. I wound down the window and the crunching of his boots grew louder. İ had visions of a rural jail cell and Austin in the impound yard. I cowered as he reached the window and demanded 'Deutsche?'

'Nein, English.'

'You car?' His dark glasses added to the threatening air.

My mouth dried out and my heart raced. 'Yes. Mine. I drove here. Belgium, Germany, Austria, Slovenia, Croatia, Serbia, Greece and now Turkey. But Turkey the best,' I grovelled and proffered my heavy file.

'No, no,' he smiled, 'we just look. It very good car.' He beamed. A few mobile phone photographs posed with Austin and I was free to climb back in and be on my way. I was still a little shaken when they flew past cheerfully hooting and waving merrily a minute later.

The other defining meeting of the day involved a wrong turn and a man with cucumbers. For some unknown reason I thought the sandy track leading off into the barren hills was, rather than the road in front of me, the route to Ihlara. Ten minutes of bouncing along, with clouds of dust filling the interior, we came to a halt, barred by a heavy-set farmer, arms crossed defiantly, in the middle of the path. He was adamant that I wouldn't pass. For a second I mulled over the idea of giving him a nudge with Austin to teach him a lesson, but instead got out all smiles, handshakes and As-Salamu Alaykum.

There was a brief stand off in Deutsch before, like the police an hour earlier, a smile broke out across his leathery, whiskered face. I was sent away with fresh directions and, for some unapparent reason, sixteen cucumbers.

Having found the young lad to let me in at the Piri Pension I pulled Austin out of their car park and drove him up a goat track followed by a comet tail of fine dust that once was part of Mount Erciyes. Pulling on the wheel I turned him into the guest compound. There was a bowel-loosening grind, a wheel spin and we slid violently sideways into the frame. The settling dust revealed, a single lazy particle at a time, that the one and a half tons of Austin appeared to be reefed on the concrete foundation of the gateway.

Coated in powder, sweat gluing my clothes to the leather seats, I put him into reverse and gently released the handbrake. I thought I was going to vomit. There was a slow anguished snarl of exhaust pipe grinding against concrete. Then thankfully we were free. A judicial wobbling of the exhaust promised everything, for the moment at least, was okay. He had a few new raffish scars cutting through his Persian blue, but that was it. Where the hell I would get an exhaust system for a 1962 British car in the badlands of Cappadocia was not one I wanted to entertain, but luck seemed to have been smiling on me for the moment. Three days later it would have its revenge.

At breakfast I ate salted eggs and jam and unleavened bread, perched gingerly on a plastic chair. The walls, tables and spare chairs were hung with ancient kilims that young bony Murat, the owner's chirpy little son, renovated through the heat of the day while he waited for the occasional tourist. Over the eggs I talked to a charming couple from Denmark about Turkey. Conny was an architect and John was a minister, whether political or pastoral I never thought to ask.

'We have been coming here for twenty years. A lot has changed. Today you're as likely to find hotels packed with Turks as with others but fifteen years ago there wasn't a soul. The rich went to their summerhouses; today the middle classes are mushrooming.' I offered them some of my cucumbers but they declined politely.

Pulling on my boots and with a stomach full of eggs

I walked out, patted Austin sat beneath the beech tree and set out to lose myself in paradise; the Ihlara Valley, a sixteen-kilometre fissure cleft from the Aksaray Plateau by the eruptions of Mount Erciyes and polished, scrupled and watered by the sapphire trickle of the Melendiz stream. Ihlara is an Eden in the relentless savagery of the stark plains above. Here, early Christians fleeing the Roman persecution sheltered from the gladius and crucifixion. Later, the now Christian Roman Byzantines honeycombed the volcanic wall with exquisite churches. Summer is long here, autumn is months away yet and the grass is bleached until it crackles. Crouched, invisible to me, were hoopoes, who lifted into the sapphire above the pistachio trees and glided away back into invisibility across the gorge. With its perfect blend of history and natural history I was utterly enamoured of it. Pausing to wash my face from the stream I stopped for lunch and lent against the trunk of a gnarled willow. Iridescent green beetles laboured through the grass like tiny absconding emeralds. Eagles thermalled above, merely specks in the blue.

Bulrushes whispered and gossiped as flycatchers darted back and forth across the Melendiz and frogs launched themselves off the muddy banks in tattoos of heavy plops and swam away all legs and determination. Lazy and sleepy with the exertion of the day and the summer I decided here and now there could be no more perfect place anywhere on earth, so I paused for lunch. The cicadas sizzled as I ate my medieval lunch of bread, cold meats, tomatoes and, of course, cucumbers.

The Agzikara Hani portico cast its wedge of shadow across Austin and I knew things weren't quite right. The uneasy feeling haunted the brief walk amongst the

Seljuk caravanserai. These halls once resounded to the laughter, noise and smells of travel and finance as camel trains set out west to the Seljuk capital of Konya or east towards Persia and China. For thousands of years camels, mules and warhorses kicked up the delicate Anatolian earth just as Austin and I did as we pulled onto the tarmac bound for Nevşehir and Goreme.

It was a short journey and the joie de vie of the days in Ihlara had taken the pressure off my shoulders. There would be no more wild goose chasing for long dead campsites. The brakes seemed a little spongy as I paused in the car park to gaze out over the surreal landscape of Goreme town. After Istanbul and the Aegean coast, Goreme is the third poster child of the tourist industry. The cones and pinnacles reach up out of the valley, monstrous fingers of volcanic rock clawing up through the earth put to use as homes, stables and, today, hotels.

To reach Kaya Camping I would turn down into the valley, pass through the town and up the other side as it was on the road to Ürgüp, a simple enough task. Yet as the road twisted down I dipped the brakes and nothing. Austin continued to gather speed. A judicial pumping did nothing as several tons of Midlands engineering continued to gather momentum. There were no hard shoulders; it was either cliff up or cliff down. With an awful grinding and juddering I double dipped the clutch snatching Austin into third. The tremor sent my files, maps, water bottle and lunch raining onto the floor. The rear view mirror, always sensitive to vibration, titled repentantly and refused to show me anything but the chaos in the foot wells. Water bottles and cucumbers rolled dangerously around under the pedals. Then with my heart pounding, fully visualising the Alpine aquaplane I carefully used the handbrake to slow me enough to drop into second. With another horrendous tremor there was a feeble sliding of the tyres and we crawled with as much dignity as we could muster through Goreme and on to Kaya Camping.

Perched high above the Kizilcukur valley the simple campsite had the best showers I'd had since leaving home. The manager, an ebullient local by the name of Yasar, thought Austin was the best thing he'd seen all day and pointed at a pitch against the far wall. Austin was parked under the olive tree and a couple of rocks were placed under the tyres. I pitched the tent, lit the stove and dragged a chair to the wall, throwing my feet up onto the wall as contented as I have ever been. And that was it for the rest of the day, I moved only to brew up or make up another pastrami, cheese and cucumber (of course) pide platter before returning, beaming ear to ear, to my roost over the valley until the skies darkened and I had to go to sleep.

In the morning I was woken by dragons. Their whispering hisses filtered into my sleepy head. The light and temperature leaking through the tent walls told me that it was barely dawn. Pulling on my jacket and woolly hat. I reluctantly left the warmth of my sleeping bag to be greeted by a still and perfect dawn blushed with the lightest reds as they paled from the blues of night. Across this fantastic canvas, floating, like silent jellyfish, were a shoal of hot air balloons, hissing and yawning. It was mesmerising. I have never had any interest in ballooning, nothing at all. But each morning, as the whooshes of ignition fuel woke me I rose and watched, captivated by the placid ballet. Now, as slowly as a tide receding, they left, departing leaving a horizon now full of the brown and yellows of a new day. A day that would involve tackling the brakes.

Between mother-in-law jokes Yasar had been persuaded to call a local mechanic. 'Old cars are the problem. Tell him to take out the part and bring it to me

172

and I will see if I can help.' This was monumentally unhelpful. I had no idea where to start with Austin's litany of mechanical complaints. But as far as the brakes were concerned it could have been the fluid, the fluid tanks, the hosing or a host of other problems. Stripping out all of Austin's braking system with virtually no tools then hitching 20 miles was ludicrous.

'I will ask about another if you like.' In the meantime I took Roger's advice and started with the brake fluid. Roger and Susan were my laid back Swiss neighbours and better travel neighbours you could never hope to find. Jovial Roger knew his way around his Land Rover and offered to lend me some tools as we stood in the cold morning assessing Austin's engine. A cockerel was starting late in the still vineyard behind us. Another Brit stood with us, breakfast beer in hand. 'I used to strip these things down as a kid. I could sort it out in about an hour for you. Yeh, it's really simple.' Brilliant, I thought. 'But I'm not going to. I'm on holiday' and with that he walked back to his pitch as if he wasn't a champion twat.

As the day began to gather strength I put my thumb out in the hope of getting a lift to neighbouring Ürgüp. A second later a clapped out jalopy came staggering around the corner almost hidden beneath a carapace of antique furniture. It was to the modern world of Turkey what a caddis fly larva is to a pond; assorted boxes, beams and fixtures covered the roof and sides as if attempting to camouflage itself in a living room.

I climbed in next to an old rascal who looked like Robert De Niro playing Rigsby in the Hollywood remake of Rising Damp. Dressed in sandals and socks, stubble and a tank top he was as threadbare and musty as the 'antiques' on the roof. We somehow communicated that I wanted to go to Ürgüp to find some fren sıvısını (brake fluid), but first he had to visit

Ortahisar to do a little business. What sort of business he was involved in was difficult to define and lay possibly somewhere between an antiques dealer, rag and bone man, conman, forger and womble. His clientele looked a great deal more likely to be involved in sex trafficking and corpse elimination services. They pulled and poked about in the tourist trinkets, blanket boxes, historic beams and mirrors. I watched from the shade of a bougainvillea cascading over the balcony above and enjoyed a fresh Anatolian peach.

We chatted, wound and juddered our way over the roundabout and into the dusty square beneath the imposing Ürgüp castle. I had worried about the integrity of Austin every other second of the trip but sat in the cacophony of that Citroen I should have given him more credit. Where Austin had a percussive ensemble this was more like listening to a brass band falling down a long flight of stairs.

'Small time, please.' I wandered across and bought some walnuts and apricots from a crumpled old man outside the mosque and retired to the shade of a bougainvillea. Families were starting to exit the mosque flashing only the faintest glances at the restaurant in the square as they made their way home or back to work. A quartet of waiters from the local köfteci eatery stalked passed, each with a shotgun slung over their shoulders, a scene that lost some of its menace with the pink t-shirts and hair gel.

There was a short whistle and I looked round. My rascal had managed to sell a pair of brass handles and was in the middle of returning everything to the roof. Once again the Citroen, with its reinstated cocoon of furniture, started with the clatter of an earthquake in a mechanic's. I climbed in and we set out for Ürgüp in search of fren sıvısını.

'Quick! Quick you must come I have something for you!' Christian had never been so animated. Over the few days the community at the campsite had developed. We had Swiss and Germans, English and Americans, Italians, Spanish and French, each travelling to the far corners of the world. I was packing Austin preparing for the morning's departure to the coast and Cyprus when the usually laconic Christian came bounding over. 'Come, come,' he said as he rushed me to a new motor home that had arrived while we had been out exploring Byzantine churches and underground cities. Sat at the dining table in the dark were Roger and Susan and two new travellers.

Mikael introduced himself and his beautiful partner Angela. 'Yah we have been working in Jordan. We have just come from Syria.'

'What?' My astonishment briefly prevailed over English politeness.

I was invited to join them at the table 'Yah, you are the Englishman with the old car.' He poured me a cup of coffee and explained that they had decided to move on and return north out of Jordan. Angela, hidden behind the steam escaping her coffee mug, said, 'Syria was no problem. It was beautiful.'

And with that tiny little innocent statement my world and my plans exploded.

By six the next morning I was tearing out of Goreme, back across the plains, desperate to reach the embassy in Ankara before it closed for the weekend. Austin simply wasn't fast enough so I had taken the bus. I could barely sit still as the salt pans flashed past. Pulling into the Şehirlerarası Otobüs Terminali I was off and across the city as soon as the coach door opened. I had spent the journey scouring the guidebook maps for the embassy in its dappled street. Alexander the Great had famously come this way and stopped to cut the Gordian knot with a simple violent solution. I had my own challenge.

It is impossible to convey the confusion and chaos in my mind. I hadn't realised just how long I had been preparing myself for the failure. The fact that I didn't even have a guidebook spoke volumes.

Out of breath I arrived at the heavily fortified Syrian compound. There was no answer to the bell. I rang it again and again and again with increasing desperation. A security guard answered. It was not good news. With stammering Turkish and English and bits of paper he communicated that the staff had all gone home for end of Ramadan celebrations, Bayram. It is the celebration at the breaking of the fast Eid-ul-Fitr, but is referred to as Küçük Bayram in Turkish. There was a holiday until Tuesday but he didn't think they would be in on Wednesday or the rest of the week. Best try the Monday after to be sure.

If I wanted to get a Syrian visa I would have to wait ten days and as I travelled back to Goreme I mused that there were far, far worse places to sit awaiting judgment. Most of the Muslim world would be closed for the next three days at least, so I should return to Roger and Susan and make the most of my extra time.

I am good at patience, but the problem lay in Nicole's imminent arrival. She had booked time off which couldn't be changed. I was supposed to meet her in Turkey on the way back. Plan B saw her meeting me in Jordan as I crossed the finish line. We hadn't planned for this. The extra week in Slovenia and now an extra ten days meant that I might, with a little luck, still meet her in Jordan as I surfaced from Syria jubilant and dashingly handsome in my coating of adventurous dust. The pessimist advised her to look at Cyprus, too.

So as the locals feasted and wished each other 'Bayramınız kutlu olsun', cleaned and laid fresh flowers at the cemeteries and the young went house to house wishing neighbours 'Happy Bayram' in return for small sweets, Turkish delight and baklava I planned and dreamed and schemed.

The clear mornings began with the yawns of the dragons and air balloon heaters while the evening closed with a veil of a million stars and dinner with Roger and Susan, Angela and Mikael. Sometimes we were joined by other travellers making their way back from or off to the four winds. Some, like Mikael and Angela were returning north and east; others were bound for the Black Sea coast, Armenia and Azerbaijan. Cycling Chris was three months into his three-year trip around the world. He was heading to Iran and along the Silk Road. Others would turn south into Pakistan and India. And then there were Roger and Susan who, having returned from Georgia, had no plans to go anywhere until the fancy took them. A hundred different escape committees all in motion and all had started with maps spread out on dining room tables or lounge carpets.

I spent long hours sat with Roger and Susan at their table or next to Austin under my tree listening to languid notes of Miles Davis taking away the heat of the day. The unearthly vista with its fairy chimneys spiking up across the valley like the rotten teeth of a monstrous titan should have looked tacky, as if it were a more money than sense folly in concrete, but burnished with the colours of Anatolian skies and given levity by the centuries of solemn prayer they were divine to gaze at all day long. The long afternoons and backdrop were perfect for catharsis. Famished and parched priests, pilgrims and holy men have all wrestled across Cappadocia in search of answers. My own was very simple and obvious. Sometimes it is only when you stop desperately searching for something that you are able to find it. Perhaps not the most refined revelation, hardly an earth shattering abreaction, but in this sweltering corner of Asia Minor it was very obvious. It was a simple thing to find the romance and excitement that my parents sought. I merely had to stop chasing about after it. Minutes, hours, days spent bent on the task of finding their physical trail had shackled and all but prohibited me from enjoying vast swathes of the journey they had revelled in. Following in their footsteps had prevented rather than fostered the pleasure and joie de vie of their adventure. Now with a blank sheet I was happier than I had been for months.

When not having pop-revelations I sat in Austin and gave tours of his eccentricities. It seemed delightful and colourful to go through his many faults, starting with the play in the steering wheel, the charm of only four gears and a set of brakes that didn't work. There would be an appreciative inhaling at the gravity of this. Moving on. There was a speedo that refused to communicate on matters of miles or miles per hour, an ambiguous fuel gauge and silent temperature and oil dials. Audiences liked the switch on the dashboard that offered no windscreen wipers or lighting for the dials at night. The finale was the windscreen cleaner fluid button that, when pushed, sprayed liquid not high on to the glass to clean away a thousand departed bugs as promised, but in the much more comical direction of all over the driver's feet. It always got a laugh. But the truth of the matter was that the brake fluid I had added did little to remedy the danger of the situation. I couldn't drive to Syria or Cyprus with only a handbrake. So in between further jokes about killing his mother-in-law Yasar heard there was a mechanic in Ortahisar. Roger, Susan and I drove Austin there and parked on the flat square and went off on foot to find the mechanic, not wanting to risk the hills and lanes of the old town.

I took longer to find the little mechanic's in the corner of the coach stop than it took to fix Austin. Finishing his chay, a short stocky man in acceptably stained overalls hobbled over. There passed a brief appraisal. Austin had a thick patina of road dust that Jim would undoubtedly approve of. I scribed 1967 in the dirt on his bonnet. '1967' could be seen in various states of degradation, as Austin had been his own blackboard over the weeks. In places 1967 could be seen tattooed in the dirt. A short mime of desperate brake pumping indicated the problem and Austin was manoeuvred over the pit. All that could be seen at the bottom of the pit was a wedge of midday sun illuminating our man's sock and sandaled feet as he shuffled back and forth. After a quick test drive and photos Austin was done. It was a massive relief. As we drove back Susan simply said 'I have driven in Austin twice today. Once with brakes and once without.'

The remainder of the sentence ticked away painfully slowly. I poured over the maps that Mikael had lent me and compared them with the 1960s map Mum and Dad had taken. The original one from the Syrian Arab Republic, Ministry of Economy, Directorate of Tourism promised 'Since the most remote times, history of the world awakened on Syrian ground; nations lived on its soil, wars were fought and arts and science developed.' If you had missed the fact that Israel was absent from the map they clarified it for you '...neighboured by: at the west, Lebanon and the Mediterranean; at the north, Turkey; at the east Iraq and Jordan and Palestine to the south.' Even today Syria is still officially in a state of war with Israel.

Sunday night just before midnight I pulled on my coat and hat and slipped out of my tent. For two days I had been nearly comatose with flu that just charged out of nowhere and flattened me. Of the previous forty-eight hours I had remained sprawled unconscious for forty-six of them. Susan and Angela took turns checking on me, opening the canvas during the day and closing it again at night. But as Sunday progressed I hauled myself up, forced some cold soup into my stomach and as the stars came out, staggered to the crossroads and overnight bus to Ankara. I collapsed onto the dimly lit seat with dreams of an almost empty Syria. All week I had fallen asleep with Angela's words in my head: 'There's no one at Palmyra'. And as the miles clicked by one by one I fantasised about waking at dawn, wrapped in my sleeping bag, leaning against Austin blinding at a dawn desert; alone and exultant in the emptiness.

Just as before I could barely wait for the bus to stop or the doors to open. An hour later, breathing heavily, I paused to gather myself and rang the bell. A small hawk like face pulled open the shutter. Placing my

180

passport on the sill I drew up my most charming smile. 'May I have a Syrian visa, please?'

A hand took the passport and instantly returned it. 'Do you have a German or Swiss passport instead?' asked the clerk.

Utterly baffled I replied I didn't.

'Then I am sorry, Mr Button, but your British government insists we are not to give you a visa. Germany or Switzerland still okay, but England and America no. I am sorry. I hope one day you will try again to visit Syria. It is very beautiful.'

Chapter Thirteen – Deep in a Dream
(Chet Baker)

A lullaby of gently rattling chains and deep diesel rumbles offered little comfort as I slept fitfully in the back of Austin. The rusting hulk of the Taşucu/Girne ferry was due to depart the fishy wharf at 12:30, but of course it didn't and we had loitered with the other lost and confused souls in the darkness; floodlit shades awaiting Charon.

Leaving what had been in '67 the proto-Hippy Trail we had pushed out of the Cappadocia steppe and through the potent Tarsus Mountains, which divide the dusty interior from the glories of the Mediterranean Sea. The endless ribbon of asphalt snaked away south, sometimes a flashing sheet of freshly finished road. 100km along, for no apparent reason, the repairs halted in a clean surgical scar and then a torture period of corduroyed ruts. The roadsides were bejewelled with broken bottles. All day long a scorching crosswind pushed us about maliciously.

The ferry didn't arrive until 12:30. There were six officials to be convinced of your worthiness to be on the ferry. 'You think this is bullshit, wait until you get to the other side,' said Raul haloed in the ugly floodlights. The cars were pulled up on the dock drowned in neon awaiting some or other official. 'I am an academic and speak three languages but you try explaining to a customs official from Idaho or Nebraska that Northern Cyprus and Cyprus aren't the same country.' The touch paper had been lit with the Colonels coup in 1967. Ten years later it would explode and eviscerate the tiny island, leaving it divided and in limbo.

'You should sleep, I'll wake you when the last one arrives.' We had been through the Port Official, an unknown official, Police, Customs Officials, Customs Inspection and a final unknown official. Who we were waiting for was a mystery to me so I thankfully nodded off.

I had no plan for Cyprus, it hadn't even been an option when I left, but along the way each and every other path had been closed and so with only a single shot left an hour later I had reversed into the hold. I had no guidebook or map and obviously no journals to guide me. Comparatively speaking Dad was hauling a horribly sick Mum across the border back into Greece by her belt straps. The next thing she would know would be a hospital physician administering an examination while dropping fag ash on her. She would be fine but it was the final nail in their trip.

The ferry was due to make land at 4am but by 10am, as I walked amongst the living dead of the ferry, there was not a merest hint of anything on the horizon. I stepped over and around bodies wrapped in tartan rugs strewn across the decking. Every last person looked thoroughly miserable. There wasn't even a smudge to suggest anything, then, cloaked in its coat of sea mist, the island materialised into the lightest watercolour stroke. It is no wonder the island is one of myth and legend, the birth place of Aphrodite and Adonis. The finest mirage curdled into a thin blue serration as the tips of the Kyrenia Mountains gently divided the sea from the sky with the finesse of a clam smile.

A pair of flying fish piloted us toward to ancient Kyrenia, or as the Turk call it, Girne.

Disembarking there were another six officials to be met and mollified. The hall was strangely hushed. The officer sat with that stony fortitude of anyone one who does business for Greeks, Turks and Cypriots. Each has to be wrangled and shackled with the formalities of law. It is a thankless task. There wasn't even a half-hearted attempt at queuing. The crossing cost me roughly £100 extra in tickets, port taxes and yet more new insurance. My insurance would only cover the southern half not the northern, Turkish, half and of course my very expensive Turkish insurance was no longer valid my having left Turkey.

Eventually with the oppressive heat beating the last ounces of sanity out of my brain we pulled off the docks and, driving on the left hand side for the first time since leaving Ramsgate months earlier, we were following a recommendation. Heading east out of Kyrenia/Girne town we searched for somewhere to pass out. The fatigue had made me blind it seemed because I failed to see a single hotel or campsite until we ran out of northern coast.

With Austin under the shade of a sea-beaten olive I turned off the engine and the gentle silence of the beach filled the car. Immediately alarm elbowed its way through the fatigue. Turning Austin off had been a mistake. Only a mouse sized click from the ignition broke the scat, scat, scat of the Med. Several more attempts did nothing to change the situation. An amateur rummage around under the bonnet did nothing except cause burns and blisters. The sweat poured off me, now that we had stopped. It forced rivulets through the grime baked to my skin. I was too tired to weep, lose my temper or express any emotion at all. So I shambled off to find lunch instead.

'We should call him Austin,' said Nicole as the kitten squirmed blissfully in her lap. Little Austin, with his bluish coat, pawed and purred like a buzz saw.

Mustafa had already said the little stray had simply arrived one morning in the workshop and decided he was staying. 'Okay, that seems like a good name. Now I think I can get the parts in Girne maybe tomorrow, maybe the day after.'

The previous three days had been full of incident and accidents. Austin had recovered enough to get to a hotel but refused to start when asked to collect Nicole from the airport at Larnaca. The instant she arrived I was overwhelmed by the huge Nicole-shaped hole that had been in me for the last few months; it had been as much a travel companion as Austin. It was impossible to express how much I had missed her and it would be days before I would allow myself to accept she wasn't simply a mirage brought on by the searing heat.

The morning after she arrived so fresh faced and beautiful we were forced to take Austin to a mechanic's. Sonny was a gent with a most splendid moustache. 'Dynamo. I thinks.' The sultry girl on the topless calendar pouted her agreement with this diagnoses. 'If I coulds not fix it or find a new ones I'll puts in an alternator. How it that? We can still maybe get you to Jordan.' He seemed to be smiling beneath that avalanche of a moustache.

But things still weren't right. When going to collect Nic from an evening's turtle conservation, Austin and I bounced down in the broadening twilight in the terrifying knowledge that if he stopped there would be no inclines for bump starts or other vehicles for a jolt of life. I completed a tour of the sandy car park as slow as I dared and on the second sweep Nic appeared saying her goodbyes. She could tell all wasn't well. When someone flings open the passenger door while driving towards you things can't be good. 'Can't stop he might stall' I yelled as I drove past. Austin bucked and flayed wildly across the dirt, his headlights strafing the bushes. Nicole and Kim stared open mouthed at me as I swung out of the gate for another circuit. Door still open we cornered and made another run like a wounded bird. As Nic said some rapid goodbyes we rolled and heaved across the uneven dirt as slowly as I dared. 'Hi Kim!' I bellowed as Nic turned and, with a hesitant jig, leapt. Thanks to the stately size of the interior and Nic's natural athleticism she easily cleared the passenger side and joined me on the driver's. Reaching down to change gear amongst a tangle of legs we made the corner and, as Nic attempted to extract herself from the gearstick and my lap, I yelled back into the darkness, 'Bye Kim, thankssss.'

The next morning Sonny directed us to a car electrician called Ezze. We failed to find him but instead found the soft-eyed Mustafa and the soon-to-be-christened Austin the cat. Mustafa had lived in Woodgreen just down the road from my grandmother it seemed before returning to Cyprus. His coffee could be used to etch steel with. It went down slowly and curled around your insides embalming them a cup at a time. Nic, with a finger to her lips, swapped my empty cup for hers while Mustafa searched for fuses. A parasailer tore across the horizon. 'I think it is the points actually. A car should have a service every three thousand miles. That should be every few year not seven week. You are lucky to make it this far.'

Austin the cat purred away cheerfully in his rascal-ish way on Nicole's lap. This wasn't the holiday I had promised her. We were supposed to meet in Turkey and for ten days we would leisurely drive back up the Aegean coast. Instead she was sat for the third day in a row in a mechanic's as gulets of visitors sailed up and down the sapphire coast enjoying their holiday.

'Its okay, I like it here. It's just like my dad's garage except cleaner. And Warren and I loved playing in there until we got caught,' she laughed. I promised that if Mustafa could get the parts we would head up to the Karpsaia Peninsular. But she wasn't too stressed, she had turtle zoologists to chat with, a tan to work on and kittens to name.

But Mustafa did a beautiful job and Austin virtually purred with new health. With his new points firing away we passed through Girne heading east to the Karpsaia Peninsular, Cyprus's handle.

It was wonderful having someone to talk to, someone else to enjoy the views and someone else to share the driving with. 'How the … have you driven this all the way here!' she said after an hour at the wheel. 'He's great in a straight line but it's like steering a bloody elephant. My arms are about to fall off.' I had got used to the vagueness of Austin's steering and the plethora of other little idiosyncrasies. I had been forced to learn in the road works of Ostend and right across the continent. Being exhausted to near-psychosis at the end of each day had become the norm.

What's that knocking? Well, then what's that one? What about this one? Pointing to the passenger foot well. I didn't have an answer for any of them. Austin's mechanical percussion had blended into the background of jazz over the weeks, and because it was jazz, the grumblings, knocks and thumps didn't have to groove with the composition, especially if I had Monk or Coltrane on.

To prove just how tough and rugged she was, Nic promptly fell sound asleep as the arid peninsular rolled past. Her blonde hair pulled and pulsed in the parched wind. I stole glances at her as she snoozed. The Cypriot sun threw a block of white from forehead to cheeks, blanching the pretty freckles that she hates so much.

The blanket I had used to cover the seat fell across her lap. With the relentless heat the leather had dried and hardened to elephant's hide. By mid-morning it was unbearable for arms and thighs.

Shepherd boys whistled in the distance, the only life as the day hummed and wobbled. Occasionally the forlorn skeleton of a new complex development, stalled in the economic crisis, rose from the earth but these petered out heading into the wilds of Karpsaia.

Hours later above a sickle of golden sand, Austin rested in the shade. Below Nic swam contentedly through the bluest waters I've ever seen, crystal sapphire and inviting. She waved up and yelled something that was lost in the wind. As the puppet master it collected up the dust making them bow and sent them on a whirling waltz across the sands. As Nic glided effortlessly across the sea in long lazy strokes, beyond her a fishing caïque with a rocking horse gait, undulating in the swell. Then there was only the horizon, blended amateurishly into the sky with the wrong brush. And beyond the horizon I imagined I could see across the white tips all the way across the sparking Med to the dusty shores of Lataika and beyond across the hills to Hama. Above the flags and placards of anti-Assad protestors my eye flies on across the stark blinding Syrian Desert to rest, with my daydreams, in the silent ruins of Palmyra dressed in dawn light. I can see Austin baked in his carapace of desert powder bouncing merrily south passed ancient Damascus, the oldest city on Earth, on across the border to rest for the night outside Amman. Austin hums along beneath a crepuscular Karak, still uttering hollow threats above the King's Highway, on to marvel at glorious Petra blushing at dawn. Finally, to the clicking and clapping boats in the harbour, he pulls in to Aqaba, hot and heroic after having travelled thousands of miles to rest his headlights on the twilight Red Sea.

'Dreaming?' Unnoticed Nicole had left the sea and stood dripping behind me. Each drop fell to darken the auburn sand black for an instant. Wrapped in a towel she opened it up and enfolded me from behind in a smooth and wet hug. Resting her dripping chin on my shoulder she stared east following my gaze to an imaginary Syria. Rivulets of cold brine trickled down my back.

'You've got one last chance' she said and kissed my neck.

'What everything?'

'Everything!'

The boot's contents were extracted item by item under the definite glare of cheap aviator glasses.

'Has it been like this all the way?' whispered Nic as she lifted the hamper out and placed it on the baking tarmac. Sweat was pouring off all three of us. Our oppressor, a creature fashioned from melting caramel, mopped his brow.

It hadn't been like this at all. The only border that even required getting out had been Turkey and even that resulted in the offer of a guided tour to the Ottoman Bosporus and a mint. Making our push to the south into the Republic of Cyprus we had been advised by ex-pats and locals alike not to waste our time queuing at the border in Nicosia, better, they said to take the scenic route west along Morfor Bay before crossing at the always empty Kato Pyrgos border.

The North Cypriots let us pass with the briefest glimpse at our documents, but the same was not true of the south. The fat little hobbit one and his colleague, a scrawny youth with the air of an amateur rapist, pored over the paperwork in detail while Nic sat in the shade sipping water politely and radiating charm and innocence while I had to scrabble under Austin with a tissue to prove the chassis number matched that of our paperwork. The tarmac scorched my exposed triceps.

As far as the southerners were concerned we were entering their lands from enemy territory and, having started there, we were in part partisan to the ongoing misery of division. To the south were the Greek Cypriots and to the north the Turkish Cypriots. With a common enemy in the Ottoman, and then the British, hostilities had remained in check, but almost the moment the island gained independence they turned on each other with stomach curdling venom.

Manipulated by barely hidden hands in Athens and Ankara, ethnic violence broke out within three years. Although an early advocate of Enosis, union with Greece, the elected Cypriot president Archbishop Makarios III chose instead to steer his new country away from the extremes of Enosis. This terrified the Turkish Cypriots, who feared an island wide surge of ethnic cleansing and the Turkish Cypriots, Taksim, the partition aligning them with Turkey. This was unacceptable to the Greek majority and so Makarios pushed for an independent Republic of Cyprus and the UN stepped in as peacekeepers. A delicate peace held for a decade while the president cultivated relationships with both the Greek junta and Turkish leaders and joined the Non-alignment Movement with Tito, Nehru and Nasser. But the enmity of the two communities was deeply rooted and he was seen by both sides as diluting their cause.

The fragility of his position became apparent when Makarios openly challenged the Ioannidis regime, accusing the Greek Colonels of sponsoring terrorism and attempting to undermine him. Greek Brigadier

Dimitrios Ioannidis now had his boot firmly on the throat of Greece and baulked at any liberalisation. With a nod from the CIA he armed and unleashed the right wing paramilitary EOKA-B, the National Guard, who swept aside the elected government. In a twist of irony Makarios fled to Paphos where his old enemies the British plucked him from the island.

This was too much for the Turks to stomach and they invaded five days later on 20 July 1974. Operation Atilla, or the Cyprus Peace Operation, was a divisive victory for the Turks and the only positive element to come out of the whole debacle was Ioannidis lost his throttle hold on Greece and it moved rapidly towards reforms and democracy, although this was little comfort to the Cypriots.

Today they remain bitterly divided although the borders have at least reopened over the last few years allowing an aging Austin Cambridge to cross and endure hours of investigation.

'Do you have a dogs?' We looked at the car, we had been there for two hours under the blistering sun. All four doors were wide open. The bonnet was up and the boot was empty. Sweat tickled down my back and Nic's mascara was threatening to run. We looked at each other, at the car and back at the guard. 'Yes, there's a fucking Afghan in the ashtray' would have been the brave reply. Instead I simply said, 'Nope, no dogs.'

'You are staying a week. We will see you in a week. You must come here' and with that we were free to leave for Paphos and our hosts.

I could see from Nic's face and the tension in her shoulders that she was not impressed with Southern Cyprus so far and I said as much. 'I'm not used to the heat for one thing.' Since Turkey I had been using the heater to draw as much of the warmth away from the engine as possible to help cool Austin. Even with the windows open and the sirocco snaking about pulling at hair and hems it was still stifling.

'And I'm not as used to this fiasco as you' she said thumbing back at the border. But that was it; I hadn't had any problems. It was hard to convince her otherwise. It was hard for me to believe as well. So far the borders had been of little challenge; however, soon fate would have her pound of flesh.

We were all hot and fed up after our Cyprian welcome so I pulled Austin into the shelter of a roadside restaurant. Nic saw my hesitation at the ignition key. 'Are you sure?' I took a gamble and the engine fell silent.

The Mediterranean, beguiling and winsome, stretched west unopposed until it grounded itself on Cretan shores. The taverna, in its azures and whites of I Kianolefki, promised respite and a respectable fish mezedes. Skinny cats pulled and stretched about the table legs and a chameleon made his haltering way across the bougainvillea. As the Greek salad, olives, green and black, and bread arrived I began to worry about Nic's view of Austin. Of the six days she had been with us there had been four visits to mechanics, a running entry and countless push and bump starts. Taramousalata, tahini, tzatziki. I felt I had to I had to restore a little faith in Austin as Nic had only seen him at his weakest. Skordalia, calamari, capers. She hadn't seen him tackle the Alps and the Sar Mountains. The storms we had battled through; the dampness and the distances that characterised Belgium, Germany, Austria and Slovenia. Halloumi, feta, fries. She hadn't witnessed the exact challenges of the pothole slaloms of Croatia, Serbia and Macedonia. Mussels, red mullet. She'd missed the adventures with the tollbooths and border crossings of Greece and Turkey. Bon appetite.

Enjoy your meal. She hadn't been with us during the bedlam of Athens and Istanbul, or the thousand miles of baking emptiness Anatolian, the dangers and the triumphs.

I wished she had.

We stayed in the bliss of Andrew's hospitality for several days. We swam in his pool and went out for meals with his wife and friends, evenings of mezedes, Italians and barbeques. Lynn agreed with Nic that I was too skinny and the pair went about returning flesh to my ribs and cheeks. We had met when they, upon returning to the hotel up north, found Nic and me trying to bump start Austin on our own a week earlier. As I gathered charge and overtook a motor scooter with a swordfish draped across the rider's lap they had invited Nic and me to visit them in Paphos. After weeks of back seat living, either mouldy in the damp or baked alive, soft beds, a full fridge and hot water was disconcerting to the point of intimidating.

After her ten day tour of Northern Cyprus' garages and Greek Cypriot customs offices Nic's stay came rushing to an end. Having someone to share the adventure, fun and hardships with had been wonderful; after all, I was retracing the steps of three friends who had been searching for the romance of the time. Yet it would seem that I had missed the point, maybe the romance was not to be found in the geography solely but in the people met along the way and, of course, those individuals foolhardy enough to go along. Both Mum and Dad had said on separate occasions 'Jimmy was great, innocent and naïve but if there were a few more people like Jim in it then it would be a much nicer world'. And suddenly, without Nic's laughter, her common sense and an unwavering desire to see what might be around the corner I was missing her within hours of her departure. WH Auden wrote that 'Man needs escape like he needs food and deep sleep' and escape was what the original journey had been about. Escape from post war London, the seeming oppression of the time. No one knew what the Summer of Love would bring, who could? The social and political paradigm shift that boiled out of the period, the Hippy Trail, racial equality and Flower Power were still in their infancy or yet to even germinate.

But in my escape I had left behind the most important element. On a journey about romance the catalyst for adventure and fun was now obvious: friendships and love. When the renowned travel writer Eric Newby was asked what he always had to take on his trips he answered 'My wife'.

Andrew drove me back to the house, where Lynn gave me a hug. A printed email was proffered with a simple 'Sorry'. Both of them had put their considered local knowledge behind my challenge to get off Cyprus and across the Middle East. The reality of any forward movement would not be one of transportation but simply politics.

That morning before Nic's tearful departure I learned that the Limmasol–Haifa ferry had been stopped. There would be no ferry to Israel from Cyprus. All those relatively easy border crossings had a penalty, and on that morning printed on A4, was the price:

Dear Mr Andrew

Our clearing agent just came back from the customs authorities.

The only way to take the car out of Cyprus is Via North (occupied part)

Either via Famagusta or Kyrineia.

Our customs authorities consider the car now as illegal in Cyprus so

They do not accept to re-export (as it is not arrive from legal port to Cyprus)

Always at your disposal for any additional information you may need.

So Austin and I were illegals. We did not exist and therefore could not move forward. What rights do ghosts have?

The only way to exist, to be resurrected or revived was to return to the North and ultimately to Turkey and home. As the carmines and scarlets of Paphos set ablaze the skies, I gathered my thoughts and as I had done a hundred times a day, everyday since leaving, I sought for a way through. The influence of that revolutionary period fifty years ago plays out in all our lives. Chaos in the Middle East had always been seen as the biggest barrier to my trip. Fifty years on, the area is still as unpredictable and volatile as ever. Yet it had been the hidden barriers that reefed my trip. The ripples radiating out of a Greece that has almost been forgotten by those who petrol bombed the riot police. Athens of 1967 rather than Damascus of today turned Austin home.

There was no whinging in '67; it was not a defeat but simply a tactical retreat. The Hippy Trail would explode and force open the passage east; fine, they would have Africa all to themselves. They still had months of adventures yet and after all it had been a test run. The Six Day War would settle down, they would save a little more money and with 'a little more focus and a little less sunbathing we'd make it to Cape Town'.

With dawn came the ritual. The oil checked, brake fluid and water confirmed. Lights working. Indictors flashing.

Turn the key and the points fire and Austin purrs.

I thanked Andrew and Lynn.

Handbrake off.
Chet Baker on.
Double-dip.
First gear.

Austin bites as the east comes alive and pulling on the heavy steering we turn for home, for autumn and for Nicole.

Epilogue

The wettest British summer on record was being elbowed aside by an autumn keen to do a better job. The news had been doom-mongering about monumental food prices after crops had gone unpollinated or rotted in the waterlogged soil. Yet somehow the sun was out and threatening a nice day.

Austin's boot yawned. The stove, tool kit and hamper were still there. The security lock for the gear stick and the petrol canisters, too. It was as if it had remained a museum since returning from Cyprus. Ultimately, Austin had been shipped home. There would have been thousands of lonely miles and several more months before I got back to Britain. There would be the staggering financial burden of the return journey, fuel, toll, accommodation and invisible special car taxes to bear. The idea of enduring the Taşucu/Girne ferry return trip alone was almost too much to contemplate. I could look forward to months of sleeping in the back of Austin each time it rained and I would have rather slammed my testicles in the door than drive back through Istanbul. No, all in all when everything was added up – time, money and sanity – it was time for Austin to take a cruise.

Briefly I had mooted the idea that I would sell Austin. After all, his job was done. Much to my surprise the backlash had been as adamant as it had been vocal. You would have thought I had been seen heading to a nearby stream with a sack of kittens and a house brick.

And so he was ennobled and became an honoured member of the family present at all Button state visits. He has been invited to drive brides to their big days, garlanded in white streamers and roses. He has been on surf trips with twinnies, quads and single fins wedged jenga-like in the back. He has even got to go to a graduation, where he basked in admiration of the recipients and benefactors alike as gowns bellowed and bustled like colossal crows. But above all he goes everywhere in company. The way it should be. He is no longer alone, stuck with a gaunt and mechanically inept guardian.

Today he went camping for the first time since returning home. 'Are you sure we need all of this stuff, it's only a two day wedding?' There was a glare that perfectly encapsulated not only my mistake but also my misplaced audacity.

Blimey this is twice what we took for three months I mumbled to Austin.

'And stop talking to the car! I heard you! The neighbours will think you're mental.' Nic came down smiling and handed me another bag for the boot. On several occasions, in Mustafa's baking garage, fishtailing through the dust of the Karpsaia peninsular and twisting through the pine-scented switchbacks of the Paphos forest, she had caught me talking to Austin. Carefully she had stepped in, keen to steer me back to the hushed water of sanity. 'I don't think he's bothered whether it's Chet, Fats or Ella.' It was going to be a long-term thing.

When the boot was packed, blankets, duvets and even a futon mattress were folded inexpertly onto the back seat, and the house was completely empty, we buckled up.

'Ready for another adventure, Austin?' Nic looked at me with a confused mixture of love and despondency. But there, just under the purr of the cylinders, behind the percussions and beneath Monk soul was the reply –

'Cool daddio, cool.'

Acknowledgements

Firstly thanks to my parents and Jimmy for making the journey in 1967 and having the miraculous forethought to keep a diary and take photographs so that five decades later I would have plenty of inspiration and material. Thanks to Susannah Marriott, Helen Shipman and Tom Scott for all their great advice and encouragement in the words department. A special thanks to Tony Perry and Don Tremayne without whom there may never have been an Austin. To everyone from Cornwall to Cyprus who embraced us with equal measures of bafflement and wide armed hospitality. But the greatest thanks is reserved for Nicole without whom this wonderful adventure would never have been possible.